influencing
like Jesus

influencing
like Jesus

15 BIBLICAL PRINCIPLES OF PERSUASION

Michael Zigarelli

with Carolyn Stanford Goss

B&H
PUBLISHING GROUP

Nashville, Tennessee

978-0-8054-4710-1

Published by B&H Publishing Group,
Nashville, Tennessee

Dewey Decimal Classification: 153.8
Subject Heading: LEADERSHIP \ JESUS CHRIST—
TEACHINGS \ PERSUASION (PSYCHOLOGY)

1 2 3 4 5 6 7 8   11 10 09 08

Dedicated to every follower of Jesus
who is serious about making a difference in the world

Acknowledgments

So many people have also positively influenced this book on influence! I am indebted to several good friends at B&H Publishing Group and LifeWay Church Resources, among them George Williams and Bill Craig who assisted in the conceptualization of this project, Len Goss, Carolyn Stanford Goss, Chris Johnson, and Kim Stanford who helpfully shaped and clarified the content, David Schrader and Julie Gwinn who lent their expertise to the titling and branding of the book, Diana Lawrence who oversaw the cover design, Betsy Wedekind, Bill Cox, Bruce Mills, and Andy Young who have so capably published the innovative video supplements for this product, and Sam House who, as usual, offered trenchant advice at every stage of the process. I've worked with a lot of publishers, but you folks are simply the best!

Thanks also to the leadership team at Charleston Southern University who afforded me enough space in my schedule to pursue this project in earnest. I'm especially grateful in this regard to my friends John Duncan, Dean of the Business School, Jim Colman, Vice President of Academic Affairs, and Jairy Hunter, President of Charleston Southern.

Also, special thanks to my long-time friend Mike Pregitzer who helped me more than he realizes to keep this resource theologically sound. This is scripture we're dealing with in this book, and Jesus in particular, so it's essential to handle this exegetical task with the utmost care. Thank you, Mike for your penetrating questions and wise counsel. This is a more faithful, more reliable resource because of you.

Indeed, God has had His hand on this project from the outset, working through many talented people who love Him, and for that I am truly grateful. Soli Deo Gloria!

Contents

Introduction

I tried to get one of my kids to eat peas the other day. It wasn't pretty. I insisted; he resisted. Locked in a stalemate, I had to pull out the influence principles covered in this book. And for this battle it looked like I might need all fifteen principles.

In the span of about thirty seconds, I mentally rifled through some options. I could use the "authority" principle ("do it because I say so"); I could use the "social evidence" principle ("look how nicely your brother is eating his peas"); I could use the "limited availability" principle ("I'm setting the timer—you have two minutes to be done"); I could take the softer approach of focusing on some benefit for him ("did you know that eating vegetables makes you grow tall?"); I could try to be likable ("you make me so proud when you eat your veggies"); I could even tell him an inspirational story ("let me tell you about some kids I saw in Brazil who spend their day begging for food").

In the end, though, I defaulted to the old, efficient standby: creating consequences. Eat or else. Since the "or else" was one part credible and two parts uncomfortable, it culminated in the boy's compliance. But in an epilogue of silent protest, he swallowed each pea like a pill, placing one at a time in the back of his throat and washing it down with a big gulp of water.

Well, problem solved—at least until next time. And unfortunately, next time was the next dinner.

Friends, this is *not* influence. I have to admit, too, that it's not uncommon for me either. When it comes to being genuinely influential and producing long-term change, I probably fail more than I succeed. That's why I've delved into Scripture to pull out God's principles of persuasion. There's got to be a better way.

As it turns out, there are a lot of better ways. God's ways. What I've discovered as I've studied and taught about influence principles over the past couple of years is that the Judeo-Christian Scriptures offer all sorts of instruction about becoming more influential. From Genesis to Revelation, an abundance of divine counsel is available to those of us who want to make a difference in the world—or at least our small corner of it.

Before I share a preview of that counsel, let me address something that's nagged at many of my Christian students who have studied influence principles. *Influence is not manipulation.* Rather, to *influence* means "to effect or to produce some sort of change in attitude, behavior, or circumstances." It's a value-neutral concept, and the influence principles in this book are also value neutral. We can choose to use these principles for good or for evil, but the principles themselves are neither good nor evil, per se.

Influence is not manipulation. *Influence* simply means "to effect or produce some sort of change in attitude, behavior, or circumstances."

Think about it this way: I can use a hammer to build a deck onto my house or to break all of its windows. The hammer itself is neither good nor bad; it's just a tool. *How I use that tool* is what's good or bad. In the same way these influence principles are simply tools; and if you learn to use them well, you'll have a significantly upgraded tool kit to be a more effective agent of change in the sphere of influence God has entrusted to you.

Here's another way we know that it's legitimate to use the influence principles described in this book: Jesus used every one of them when he walked among us.

That's an important starting point. It's relatively easy to find examples of persuasion in the Bible—examples of people who have been influential through whatever means available—but that's not Bible study. That's simply proof-texting, and it can lead us to some erroneous conclusions about what's permissible in God's eyes. So as a guardrail against that, my operating assumption in doing research for this book has been this: if Jesus did it, then we can be pretty confident that it's OK for us to do it, too.

You'll find a lot of examples in this book from people other than Jesus—examples from Paul, Nathan, Solomon, Nehemiah, Daniel, and so on—but you'll find no influence principle covered that we cannot infer directly from Jesus' teaching or actions.

God Wants You to Be an Influencer

You might be one of those folks who ask another good question about this topic: *why study influence in the first place?* Let me tell you, it's about so much more than peas at the dinner table. In fact, that example is trivial compared to the enormity of God's invitation in this area. God calls us to be influencers in several different realms, every day of our lives.

Did you ever consider that? God has given us a Great Commission, a mandate to make disciples, to encourage people to consider the claims of Jesus Christ, and to make a persuasive case for Christ through who we are and what we say. *That's a call to influence.*

And beyond this Great Commission, God gives us a Cultural Commission, an instruction to shape our workplaces, our schools, our public policies, our media, and our entire society in ways that please him. There's nothing less than a cultural war going on out there—a battle for our hearts and minds and for the hearts and minds of our children—and God doesn't want us Christians on the sidelines in that battle. He wants us on the front lines; and, frankly, he wants us to win those battles. *That's a call to influence.*

And even beyond the Great Commission and the Cultural Commission, God gives us a Domestic Commission to train up our kids in the way they should go (Prov. 22:6)—to teach them to love God and neighbor—and to be salt and light to our spouses and to others in our household, gently but effectively shepherding them ever closer to God. *That's a call to influence.*

God gives us a Great Commission,
a Cultural Commission, and a
Domestic Commission. Each of these
is a call to influence.

God gives us opportunities all around us every day to influence people and circumstances. Whether you're a concerned citizen writing a letter to the editor, or a pastor stepping into the pulpit, or a teacher instructing your class, or a stay-at-home mom shaping your children's worldview, or a manager trying to grow your organization or lead your people God's way, or an activist trying to convince your legislature to change a law, or an evangelistically-minded believer encouraging someone to consider seriously the claims of Jesus Christ, or even if you're just a dad trying to get your kids to eat their peas, everyday influence opportunities abound. Thanks be to God that he hasn't left us on our own to figure out how to do this stuff! He's revealed to us in Scripture more than a dozen influence principles, and he gives us his Holy Spirit to empower us to do it successfully.

That empowerment is actually the launch point for this book's subject. It's Principle 1. Indeed, we can choose to use these influence principles in our own strength, but there's a better way. As with everything in life, God wants us to co-labor with him and to rely on him to make a real difference in this world. Being a change agent is not just another thing for our to-do list. It's a central part of our purpose. It's a divine calling and even a sacred way of life, a habit of being God's conduit to get people onto God's agenda. He's the influencer; we're just the vessels, using his principles his way to do his work.

How This Book Is Organized

Let me offer you a quick road map to how I've structured this book. Each chapter is a short, focused discussion of one of the fifteen principles I've discovered about how Jesus influenced people. You can read this book alone and find much that you can put into practice. Maybe you absorb material best where you can reflect on it in a quiet setting.

Or maybe you just want to study with a partner. I strongly encourage you to consider reading and studying it in a collaborative way, even if it's just two or three of you together, because you'll benefit *immeasurably* from others' ideas about how to use these principles in your life.

At the end of each chapter, I'll offer a "For Reflection" section that contains questions for you to think about. This section will help you get practical and personal because: the more personally applicable the material, the more learning and growth takes place.

Therefore, there will be a strong focus on applying each influence principle *to your specific influence challenges.* I encourage you to get a notebook and to journal some responses to the reflection questions so that you can solidify your understanding of these principles.

May I challenge you to reflect on these questions as your first journal entry:

- Is there a person or two in your life whom you'd like to influence in some meaningful way?
- Is there a particularly difficult conflict that's been festering for a long time, one for which you've not been able to make much progress?
- Is there a big opportunity before you that requires you to be more persuasive than you've been in the past?

By the time you finish this book, you'll have at least fifteen fresh ideas for how you can be a better influencer in that situation and with that person or persons. In short, you'll have an "influence plan," so you don't have to keep approaching that situation the same way anymore.

> You'll be able to apply each influence principle to your specific influence challenges so you can take away a personal "influence plan."

Sound intriguing? I hope so. But for some I've taught, it sounds a little strange. "Plan my influence?" they ask. "Does it really have to be that premeditated? That much work? That formal?"

If you're wondering the same thing, consider this: When things matter, we often create some sort of plan. Can you imagine wanting to send your kids off to college someday without creating a financial plan to do so? Can you imagine a builder starting construction without an architectural plan? Or a professional coach stepping onto a field without a game plan? Or a business trying to grow without a strategic plan? Or a general engaging the enemy without a battle plan? Or a teacher stepping up to the lectern without some sort of lesson plan?

When something's important, we plan. So why do we approach our significant influence challenges without an influence plan?

We shouldn't, and we don't have to. To get you started, in the back of this book you'll find an easy-to-use but surprisingly powerful Influence Planning Worksheet. Try it. Work through it one time to construct a new path forward in a conflict or opportunity you're currently facing. If you're serious about being a more godly influencer—at home, at work, at church, in the neighborhood, in the mission field, in the classroom or the courtroom or the board room—get serious about planning an influence strategy.

Influence matters. It matters a lot because God wants us to be influencers. He'll help you with this if you sincerely ask him. So let's turn to that very issue now—the issue of co-laboring with God—in Principle 1.

PART 1

Before You Ever
Say a Word

Thank you for embarking on this journey with me! It's my hope and prayer that God will do something special in your life through *Influencing like Jesus*, so that you can do some special things for him in return.

The first three influence principles that we'll cover in this book might be more accurately called "pre-influence principles." They are three things we should do before we ever say a word to try to influence somebody or some situation.

Did you ever think about that? So often we simply go charging in with our solutions or arguments, having done little groundwork in preparation. Whether we're seeking to resolve a conflict, to change somebody's mind, or to encourage someone to alter their behavior, we often just react, defaulting to whatever influence approach we normally take.

Not a great idea. That's a little like taking a test without studying for it.

We can do better than this, and God wants to help us to do better. *Before we ever say a word to try to influence someone, we should do at least three things that he teaches us in Scripture,* as we'll see in the next three chapters:

- Pray for change.

- Be a person others will follow.
- Know your audience.

This has the potential to be an important journey for both of us, and I'm grateful you're taking the time to join me. God wants us to be influencers, as we said in the introduction to this book, and he's about to show us how to do that.

— PRINCIPLE 1 —

Pray for Change

This principle may be so self-evident that it seems trite even to say it. It's like a throwaway line, an obligatory statement all Christian authors or pastors must make to assure their audience that they're one of the faithful. Or maybe it's one of those things Christian publishers automatically include in their practical resources lest the resources seem too secular. Whatever the reason, it's little more than stating the obvious, right?

But humor me. Let me say it anyway, just to get it on the record: *Prayer changes things*. It's the starting point for influence. We shouldn't go charging ahead independently and self-sufficiently but, instead, co-labor with God to persuade people. After all, God does the changing. We're merely the instruments he's using to effect the change.

In fact, Scripture says that "in everything, through prayer and petition with thanksgiving, let your requests be made known to God" (Phil. 4:6). *In everything*. That includes our attempts to influence people and circumstances. And it's modeled throughout the Bible. There are countless examples.

The patriarchs prayed for change. Genesis says, for example, that "Abraham prayed to God, and God healed Abimelech, his wife, and his female slaves" (Gen. 20:17).

Moses prayed for change. When God had heard enough complaining from his people, he sent fire to surround their camp. But Moses "prayed to the LORD, and the fire died down" (Num. 11:2).

The prophets prayed for change. *A lot.* Jeremiah prayed so much that one time God even insisted he stop interceding for the people of Judah, apparently so that God's plans would go forward! (Jer. 7:16).

Jesus himself teaches us to pray for change. He says, "Keep asking, and it will be given to you."

The psalmists prayed for change—to be restored in their relationship with God (e.g., Ps. 51), to be healed (e.g., Ps. 6), for safety (e.g., Ps. 57), and even that God would strike down their enemies (e.g., Ps. 109).

Jabez prayed for a change in the size of his territory—that God would "extend my border"—and Scripture says that "God granted his request" (1 Chron. 4:10).

Jesus' brother James tells us directly to pray for change, explaining that "you do not have because you do not ask" (James 4:2) and that a prayer offered in faith can make a sick person well (James 5:13–15).

Most instructively, Jesus himself teaches us to pray for change. He says, "Keep asking, and it will be given to you" (Matt. 7:7). He tells his disciples, "Anything you ask the Father in My name, He will give you" (John 16:23). He modeled the principle, too, praying that God would transform us into the kind of people who would draw many to him (see John 17:21).

If it's so clear that prayer changes things, and if so many of us Christians desire change, why do so *few* of us have a healthy and active prayer life?

All of these prayers—and so many others in the Bible—are prayers to influence people and circumstances. Indeed, prayer changes things. But here's the problem: *if it's so clear that prayer changes things, and if so many of us Christians desire change in ourselves and others, why do so few Christians have a healthy and active prayer life?*

A Quick Confession

OK, confession time: My question comes from uncomfortable firsthand experience with the problem. Please don't misunderstand me: I believe that every verse cited above is true. I believe that they come from God himself, through inspired writers of his choosing. Still, though I'm a Christian and even a teacher of Christians, I've wrestled for years with this question of whether prayer changes things. And here's the kicker: the more Christians I talk to at the heart level, the more I realize that I'm not alone. In fact, those of us who struggle with the nature of prayer may even be in the majority.

I've seen some studies that support my unscientific conclusions. But you may not need empirical evidence to relate to what I'm saying. Maybe you're wanting to ask this same question, or you know someone else who might be. If so, let's look together at a root cause of our disbelief— the reason we neglect to pray for change.

Why We Don't Pray for Change

Why is it that churchgoing, Bible-believing Christians— people who nod at verses like "Keep asking, and it will be given to you" (Matt. 7:7)—still neglect to invite God into our attempts to persuade people? What's the root cause? Is it just that in our hurry we forget to talk to God? Sometimes, perhaps, but I think the problem runs far deeper than dashing. More likely, it's a result of being marinated daily in a culture of disbelief.

Although the vast majority of Americans believe in God, the majority of that majority also thinks we can't know much about God. After all, they reason, how can you *really know* anything about the supernatural? Yes, we believe God exists, and we may even be able to infer some things about God's power and transcendence from looking at his creation. But whether he actually *gets involved* in his creation and *listens and responds* to our petitions, who can say? The Bible? It makes claims about all these things, but even among Christians fewer than one in three even believes that moral absolutes exist! So much for God revealed through Scripture. So much for knowing God. Relativism rules, even in the church.[1]

This is what I mean by "a culture of disbelief." We live in a society where the predominant worldview is secularism, a presumption that says it's not possible to know anything *with certainty* about the supernatural. After a couple hundred years of this cultural drift, it's no surprise that the disbelief has penetrated our churches.

Experiment with this premise, if you'd like. See for yourself. To ten people who are not Christians, say something about the supernatural realm—something like, "We can know God's will for our lives," or "God speaks to us," or "Satan is a liar." Then count how many blank stares you get in response. I'll bet there'll be at least seven. Replicate this experiment with Christians, and you'll probably get at least five.

Now stay with me because this takes us back full circle to the issue of prayer. If we live in a culture that's agnostic about whether God is truly knowable, then we live in a culture that's agnostic about whether prayer changes things. And as you probably know, we see this doubt reinforced every day through TV shows, movies, the print media, music, public education, and even many of our laws. Is it any surprise, then, that we also are infected? It's such a gradual poisoning, though, that we don't even realize it's happening.

Until, that is, someone asks us about the quality of our prayer life, and we're suddenly too embarrassed to be honest. *How did that drift happen?* we wonder. *Why don't I communicate with God more? Why don't I pray for change anymore?*

Maybe, just maybe, it's because we've been slowly conformed to that ubiquitous culture of disbelief. Maybe we no longer truly believe (if we ever did) that prayer makes a difference in what happens in our lives, and maybe we've ingested so much of this cultural toxin that it's transformed our spiritual DNA.

So maybe, just maybe, it's time to allow God to transform it back, once and for all.

A Long-standing Problem, a Timeless Solution

Let me underscore that this skepticism about the power of prayer is a long-standing problem, not just a contemporary one. It's exemplified clearly in one story told in the book of Acts. Peter is in prison and about to be executed. His friends are praying for his release—praying but apparently not fully believing that their prayers will make a difference. Look at the text:

> On the night before Herod was to bring him out
> [for execution], Peter was sleeping between two
> soldiers, bound with two chains, while the sentries
> in front of the door guarded the prison. Suddenly
> an angel of the Lord appeared, and a light shone in
> the cell. Striking Peter on the side, he woke him up
> and said, "Quick, get up!" Then the chains fell off
> his wrists. "Get dressed," the angel told him, "and

put on your sandals." And he did so. "Wrap your cloak around you," he told him, "and follow me." So he went out and followed, and he did not know that what took place through the angel was real, but thought he was seeing a vision. After they passed the first and second guard posts, they came to the iron gate that leads into the city, which opened to them by itself. They went outside and passed one street, and immediately the angel left him.

Then Peter came to himself and said, "Now I know for certain that the Lord has sent His angel and rescued me from Herod's grasp and from all that the Jewish people expected." When he realized this, he went to the house of Mary, the mother of John Mark, where many had assembled and were praying. He knocked at the door in the gateway, and a servant named Rhoda came to answer. She recognized Peter's voice, and because of her joy she did not open the gate, but ran in and announced that Peter was standing at the gateway.

"You're crazy!" they told her. But she kept insisting that it was true. Then they said, "It's his angel!" Peter, however, kept on knocking, and when they opened the door and saw him, they were astounded. (Acts 12:6–16)

"You're crazy"? "They were astounded"? To be candid, I might have said the same thing and felt the same way. And so would many longtime Christians that I know.

That's just the point. We don't pray because we doubt, and even when we do pray, we doubt. Scripture teaches us, though, that if we want to make more of a difference in this world, whether it's in the lives of a million people or only one, it begins by rebuking this doubt (see James 1:5–7; Heb. 11:6), by asking God's forgiveness, by letting him cleanse us of our cultural contamination, and by believing his Son's teaching that prayer changes things. Jesus said about prayer that anyone who "does not doubt in his heart, but believes that what he says will happen, it will be done for him" (Mark 11:23). This, then, is our timely solution to the timeless problem of disbelief: ask God to give us a confident expectation that our prayers matter.

> Jesus said about prayer that anyone who "does not doubt in his heart, but believes that what he says will happen, it will be done for him."

Is this something you need to deal with before going any further? Do a quick self-assessment to find out. Reflect back on your recent attempts to persuade somebody of something. How much of a role did prayer play in that attempt? Was communication with God part of your process, or do you normally go at this alone? In the same way, watch yourself over the next week or so, especially a few days after reading today's study. Observe your approach to persuading people and see whether you're habitually asking for God's guidance.

What we do exposes what we believe. So look at what you do and then, if necessary, do whatever it takes to align your beliefs with God's Word. Remember, influence does not begin with a set of persuasion principles or with a set of tactics or even with honing your arguments until they're airtight: it begins by seeking God and inviting him to do the influencing through you.

For Reflection

Pray for change. Each day brings abundant opportunities to put this principle into practice. Consider how widely applicable it is. On any given day, you might want to:

- Encourage your kids to behave better.
- Persuade your mate to change his or her mind about something important.
- Influence your boss to be fairer or nicer or more generous.
- Convince a teacher to change his or her approach to educating your child.
- Secure a refund from a customer service representative.
- Invite a sibling or friend to accept the claims of Jesus.
- Petition God to end a war or eliminate abortion or install leaders who will honor him.
- Achieve a personal change of heart so you can finally enjoy inner peace.

Indeed, every day we want to be influential. So let me encourage you to try something practical: identify the most pressing situation in your life where you'd like to see some sort of change—where you'd personally like to be more influential. Pick something significant, perhaps a situation that you've been trying to affect for years, a situation where you need some fresh insight into how to be more persuasive. Record in your notebook or journal what your personal challenge is.

Now, with that as your target, look for opportunities to work on this situation as you explore the influence principles that follow Principle 1, "Pray for change." If you prefer, pick two or three influence challenges instead of one. Regardless of the number, your goal should be to develop a practical plan of action full of new ideas about how to have more influence in the situation you've identified.

Lastly but most essentially, before you move on to something else today, take the first step toward greater influence and *pray for the changes you'd like to see in this situation, believing that God will intervene.* And beyond that, commit to continuing this conversation with God throughout your reading of this book. Influence toward permanent transformation begins here, this very moment, with these very prayers.

Be a Person Others Will Follow

Tippy. That's what he called the dog. It was a little thing, only about eight inches high, with some characteristics of a short-haired terrier. But I think it was a mutt.

Regardless, on this fateful day, Tippy ran out to greet me and Cinnamon, my always-happy-to-see-you golden retriever, as we took a walk around the neighborhood. Unlike Cinnamon, Tippy's owner seemed to be one of those never-happy-to-see-you types. As his dog darted out from the garage to say "Hi," the guy angrily yelled: "Tippy, get back here!"

The dog ignored him and met us with his stubby tail in overdrive. Cinnamon and Tippy began some kind of dog greeting ritual like old friends, despite this being their first meeting and despite their David and Goliath size difference. Then the real Goliath in this story roared again: *"Tippy!"*

It was bloodcurdling—sort of a "come here or I'll kill you!" tone. And Tippy knew it as he took a sheepish but only momentary glance back. He'd no doubt heard it before, but Cinnamon was apparently too intriguing for this little pup to comply.

Then, with neighbors now peeking out their windows and doors, the owner turned it up yet another notch: "Tippy! Get over here *now*!" That one left even my ears ringing since he was practically right next to me by this point. He grabbed his dog by the collar and slapped it across the face, yelling something about listening the first time, even salting it with profanity. The poor dog was sent rolling by the force of the slap, and finally, sadly, slinked back to the garage.

The guy apologized for his "bad dog," and I told him it was OK—the dog was just coming out to say hello. What I wanted to say was: "Hey, Pavlov, no wonder your dog doesn't want to come to you. When he does, he gets whacked!" But I kept that little nugget to myself, lest Cinnamon and I get whacked, too.

I wonder from time to time how poor Tippy is doing. I'm half expecting him to show up at my door with a backpack and bus ticket. I also wonder how my neighbor's doing. I don't see him much since he's on the other side of our development, but I have seen him, in a sense, in other people I know. And sometimes, I'm embarrassed to say, I occasionally see him in my own mirror.

A lot of us try to influence others through anger. Parents do it, older siblings do it, spouses do it, bosses do it, coaches do it, drivers do it, sometimes even pastors do it. And let's face it, it works to some extent. Especially when one person has more power than another person, communicating anger can lead to compliance. But don't miss this: It may lead to compliance, but it never—*never*—leads to commitment. It is not a pathway to long-term influence.

> There's an inextricable link between who we are and how much influence we command.

Why? Because we don't follow angry people. We don't respect them; and, truth be told, we seldom even like them. Instead, we're more likely to follow joyful people. Upbeat and positive people. Encouragers and people who have compassion for us. Gentle people. People who are humble. People we trust and around whom we feel safe. And people who are excellent at what they do.

That's a diverse list, but the point is that Principle 2 is only in small part about anger. The broader lesson is that there's an inextricable link between who we are and how much influence we command. Being a world-class influencer begins by depending on God through prayer, which is principle 1; and it continues on that foundation by being the type of person others are willing to follow.

Dirty Sponges Clean Nothing

Let me explain that a little more since it's so critical that we get this right. It's a reality that you've likely seen in your own persuasion attempts: We can be our own worst enemy when it comes to influence. We torpedo our efforts by acting in a way that turns people off to our message.

Like I said, this is about so much more than anger. I had a dentist, for example, who told me during one of those classic monologues to the mute that he had gotten some insider information on a new, top-secret technology that a dental company was about to roll out. So based on that tip (an illegal tip, mind you, and he knew it), he bought lots of stock in that company, netting him "a 1,000 percent profit" of about thirty grand. "Not bad for a week's work!" he chuckled to his captive audience.

After he was done regaling me with his market killing and his tooth filling, he made a quick sales pitch for me to bring my four kids to see him. "Sure, I'll sign them right up," I thought, amused by how someone so smart could be so dumb. You do illegal things and then brag about them, and I should trust you with my kids? His 1,000 percent profit story culminated in 0 percent influence with me.

The problem occurs at least as much at home as it does out in the marketplace as we say and do things that contravene the very lessons we're seeking to teach our kids, our spouse, or anyone else to whom we're trying to be a light. Know the feeling? It's an awful one, especially for those of us who take our Domestic Commission seriously.

Stay with me because there's a lot at stake here. The many principles we cover in this book for persuading those around us will get us nowhere unless we're becoming the type of person others will follow. Dirty sponges clean nothing. Usually they just make more of a mess.

That doesn't mean we have to be perfect in order to be effective influencers. But it *does* mean that we should remain constantly aware that those we seek to influence will filter our words through our behavior. If the latter does not match the former, then little will change.

Five Qualities of a Godly Influencer

There are dozens of personal characteristics that cause people to be receptive to our influence. In study after study, honesty and trustworthiness top the list, usually followed by qualities such as being competent, courageous, supportive, and caring, and having a clear vision for the future.

The research is little more than an affirmation and an echo of what we see in Jesus. Perhaps that's why he could simply say "follow me" and people would drop everything.

Sound like anyone you know? Hint: Think back about two thousand years—or to the last time you read the Gospels. Interestingly, such research is little more than an affirmation and an echo of what we see in Jesus. Perhaps that's why he could simply say, "Follow me" and people would drop everything.

But for the moment let's broaden our scope to the whole counsel of God. What personal attributes, as described in Scripture, lay the most solid foundation for our influence? Though this is certainly not an exhaustive list, let me suggest these five attributes as a start:

1. Be Authentic

No one follows a hypocrite (except, perhaps, out of curiosity). Hypocrisy is the antithesis of influence, and it's the antithesis of God's will. Sure, we're each guilty of it to some extent, but that's because we're each human. It doesn't have to be nearly as bad as it is though.

God calls each of us to be authentic, to be a genuine follower. He doesn't expect perfection but faithfulness, a co-laboring with him to walk our talk, to be the same in public and in private, and to model the way for others. He invites us to narrow the belief-behavior gap that has plagued us for years and finally to take seriously his bedrock teaching that "whoever claims to live in him must walk as Jesus did" (1 John 2:6 NIV).

2. Be Compassionate

Why were people so drawn to Jesus? Why were they so deeply influenced by him? Many reasons, as we'll see throughout this book, but arguably the paramount reason is this: Jesus had compassion on them.

Over and over again in the Gospels, we hear words to this effect:

- "Moved with compassion, Jesus touched their eyes. Immediately they could see, and they followed Him" (Matt. 20:34).
- "Moved with compassion, Jesus reached out His hand and touched him. 'I am willing,' He told him. 'Be made clean'" (Mark 1:41).
- "He saw a huge crowd and had compassion on them, because they were like sheep without a shepherd. Then He began to teach them many things" (Mark 6:34).
- "He had compassion on her and said, 'Don't cry.' Then He came up and touched the open coffin, and the pallbearers stopped. And He said, 'Young man, I tell you, get up!'" (Luke 7:13–14).

As you see, compassion is more than empathy, more than feeling sorrow or pity for someone. Compassion is *empathy in action*, a feeling that moves one to actual service. This stands in sharp contrast with the posture of the religious leaders of Jesus' day, who "tie up heavy loads that are hard to carry and put them on people's shoulders, but they themselves aren't willing to lift a finger to move them" (Matt. 23:4).

Why were people so drawn to Jesus? Why were they so deeply influenced by him? One of the major reasons was this: Jesus had compassion on them.

We'll cover Jesus' compassion in more detail in Principle 5, but for now, recognize that compassion doesn't come naturally to everyone. And to make matters worse, there's no quick fix—it's not easy to cultivate if you don't already have it. But since a hallmark of the Christian is care, we clearly need to work toward a more compassionate spirit.

How? Admittedly, I struggle with this a lot. I stand with those who aren't exactly hardwired to serve. I have different DNA, I guess, different gifts. What I've learned through the struggle, though, is this: as I grow closer to God, I increasingly see people the way he sees them, and compassion—even for the people who don't like me—makes a surprise appearance.

3. Be Honest

In addition to being the number one influence trait in contemporary surveys, honesty is a biblical mandate. God's Word promotes honesty as an ideal from the Mosaic Law through the Proverbs and on to Jesus' words in his Sermon on the Mount:

- "Do not give false testimony against your neighbor" (Exod. 20:16).
- "Don't let your mouth speak dishonestly, and don't let your lips talk deviously" (Prov. 4:24).
- "But let your word 'yes' be 'yes,' and your 'no' be 'no'" (Matt. 5:37).

The ideal is also driven into us from the earliest days of our memory—at home, at school, at church—but ironically, it's driven right back out of us later in life by our narcissistic, pragmatic, it's-all-about-me culture. We're exposed regularly to people who say they're going to do one thing but then do another just because it's expedient to do so. And, just as the apostle Paul predicts when he says "bad company corrupts good character" (1 Cor. 15:33 NIV), we can find ourselves imitating their behavior.

Perhaps that's why honesty and trustworthiness and credibility are endangered species these days. Perhaps that's also why those who actually embody these virtues, despite the occasional cost, shine brighter than ever and gain the lion's share of influence.

4. Be Excellent

Unfortunately, we don't hear enough today about the theology of excellence. It's not complicated, though. God wants us to do everything for him. *Everything.* Not one thing is exempt. The jobs we perform, the work we do around the home, the way we drive, the way we live our lives moment to moment—what we look at, how we think, what we buy, how we use our tongues, and so on—is to be done first and foremost for God. So why should our efforts ever be anything less than our best? How is mediocrity ever an option for a believer?

It's not. It surely wasn't for an influencer like Daniel, whose work and intellect were so excellent that he was installed as prime minister under several foreign kings. It wasn't for David, either, as excellence in battle led to his ultimately being crowned king of Israel.

Then there's Joseph. Through excellence in dream interpretation as well as in administration, Joseph gained and maintained a position of power and influence in Egypt.

And of course, through unprecedented excellence Jesus captivated minds and captured hearts: "The crowds were astonished at His teaching, because He was teaching them like one who had authority, and not like their scribes" (Matt. 7:28–29).

Paul writes, "Whatever you do, do everything for God's glory" (1 Cor. 10:31). Love God enough to work for him in all things, excelling at everything to which you put your hand. When we follow God this way, people naturally follow us.

5. Be Gentle

Overlooked by many, this "fruit of the Spirit" characteristic is a surprising and delightful pathway to persuasion. When we think of influencers, we often think of charismatic leaders like generals or politicians or coaches or pastors who speak forcefully on the major issues of the day. But Scripture doesn't draw any connection between charisma and influence. Instead, it calls us to influence through gentleness, despite whatever hardwiring we may have to the contrary.

Jesus' first adjective to describe himself is "gentle" (Matt. 11:29). Look at the vast majority of his interactions. He influenced people with patience—with a gentle nudge, a loving touch, a warm smile, a word aptly spoken. This was his communication style, not flamboyant speeches or angry diatribe. Indeed, when confronting the religious hypocrites of the day, he was forceful and even harsh, but that was a special case that demanded a different approach.

Look at the vast majority of Jesus' interactions. He influenced people with patience—with a gentle nudge, a loving touch, a warm smile, a word aptly spoken.

Would you like a more explicit connection between gentleness and influence? Consider this counsel from the book of Proverbs:

"A ruler can be persuaded through patience,
and a gentle tongue can break a bone." (25:15)

"A gentle answer turns away anger,
but a harsh word stirs up wrath." (15:1)

Through gentleness and patience, our wisdom book says, we can persuade those in key leadership positions, and we can diffuse an escalating situation. The trait comes in handy at other times as well, like when we evangelize (see, for example, 1 Thess. 2:7; 1 Pet. 3:16) or disciple others (see Gal. 6:1). Not exactly trivial matters to be fumbled away.

Maybe gentleness is simply part of the disposition that God gave you. If so, thank him regularly for this tremendous gift! But if it's not part of your innate gift mix, why not commit to working on this, perhaps by road-testing for yourself today this approach to influence? With advocates like Jesus, Solomon, Peter, and Paul, we can be pretty confident that it'll work.

To Be an Influential Christian, Be a Likable Christian

Overall, much of what we've said here could be summarized in two words: *Be likable.* Do you see that this is a thread that runs through Principle 2? As we work persistently toward the five biblical attributes described above—authenticity, compassion, honesty, excellence, and gentleness—as well as other virtues, we become much more likable people. That's important for any would-be influencer since people are more prone to be influenced by those they like than by those they do not like.

Sounds pretty logical, right? But it's not something that's particularly emphasized in most Christian communities. Think about it: When was the last time you heard from the pulpit or from a Christian magazine about the value of "being likable"?

This influence principle is Christianity 101, which makes it such a natural fit for us. As we encourage people, as we're generous with our compliments, as we drive courteously, as we give charitably, as we smile a lot, and as we're grateful and positive, we not only model Jesus for those around us; we also become the type of people others will follow—likable Christians who have earned the right to speak meaningfully into others' lives.

For Reflection

Principle 2, "Be a person others will follow," says that we're influenced by people whom we like, trust, respect, and who walk the talk. Where have you seen this principle in operation? Jot down in your notebook some examples of people from your life who model this principle.

Think about the greatest influence challenge or challenges in your life. Ask yourself: "What characteristics do I need to demonstrate to earn the right to be heard in this situation? Also, are there others whom this person likes and trusts who could be the influencers?"

— PRINCIPLE 3 —

Know Your Audience

Did you ever find it odd that there are four Gospels? And that they seem so different in so many ways? Surely God could have communicated everything he wanted to tell us in one Gospel, right? So why four?

The answer helps us understand an essential principle of influence. God knew his audience. Or, more precisely, God knew his *audiences*—the four audiences he wanted to reach with the most important message of all time.

If you think about the first century AD, whom would you have to influence if you wanted to launch a worldwide movement? First of all, the Greeks—the intellectual heavyweights of the day—and second of all, the Romans, the political heavyweights. Beyond that, God wanted to communicate the Good News to his chosen people, the Israelites, as well as to all people everywhere, across the generations, to advance his Great Commission.

Four audiences, each requiring a different approach to be persuaded that God's Son had come to die for them. Same truth message, four different packages.

Now watch this. It fits like a glove. For the Greek audience, God selected one of their own as his inspired writer, a man named Luke. Because the Greeks' worldview was so humanistic, so sure that man is the measure of all things, Luke puts a heavy emphasis on Jesus' humanity. For example, Luke takes the time to explain the details of the Savior's birth, whereas the other Gospel writers do not.

Luke's genealogy traces Jesus' lineage all the way back to Adam, linking Jesus to the first man (Matthew's genealogy, by contrast, stops at Abraham). And Luke's favorite title for Jesus, tellingly, is "Son of Man," a term used three times more by Luke than by John, who, as we'll see in a minute, puts his emphasis on Jesus' divinity.

For the Roman audience, and even more specifically, for the persecuted Roman Christians who would hold the key to the future of that church, God inspired a man named John Mark to write the Gospel of Mark. As a result, we see Mark diving right into the story of Jesus' ministry, moving quickly through it (notice the brevity of Mark's Gospel and that almost everything in it happens "immediately"), and emphasizing Jesus as a suffering servant for all of humanity—a person with whom persecuted people could clearly identify.

For his chosen people God tapped Matthew to write. This audience would insist on proof that any alleged Messiah fulfill the prophecies in their Scriptures, what we Christians call the Old Testament. So Matthew filled his message with more than four dozen references to these prophecies. Moreover, Matthew traces Jesus' ancestry to Abraham, the father of the Israelite nation, rather than to Adam, whose name carried far less weight with this group.

And finally, to all people of all times, God sends John. Notice that John's Gospel is strikingly different from the other three, in part, I think, because the target audience is so different. John's audience is vast, diverse, and hungry for a connection to God and a pathway to salvation. So for twenty-one chapters John presents Jesus as just that— a divine and eternal Savior, a Redeemer for all. In doing so, he pens a masterpiece that even two thousand years later we can hand off to anyone anywhere in the world as an introduction to Jesus, to the Christian faith, and to the promise of salvation.

Fascinating, don't you think? And for our purposes in this study, fascinatingly instructive, since it teaches us the importance and arguably the *mandate* to know our audience before we communicate with them.

What *We* Find Convincing Will Not Necessarily Convince Others

Different audiences, different approaches to communication. It's a principle of persuasion we'd be wise to remember before we ever say a word to the person we're seeking to influence.

Jesus did. This is one of the reasons he taught through storytelling. Stories reach people of every education level and life situation, and especially when the stories—like Jesus' stories—are about things the audience understands well: farming, business dealings, marriage festivals, wayward children, and so on. Stories are also effective because they keep people listening to the end (not a minor consideration), the lessons stay with people long after the story is over, and they're easily transferable from person to person, family to family, generation to generation. Jesus, knowing his contemporary and future audiences, taught in a way that they (and we) would actually learn.

> Jesus, knowing his contemporary and future audiences, taught in a way that we'd actually learn.

Telling audience-appropriate stories is such an important approach to influence that we'll spend all of principle 7 focusing on it. But it works only when we respect the broader principle behind it: learn as much as you can about the person you're trying to influence *before* you go charging in with your brilliant insights and rationales. *What would convince him or her is not necessarily what would convince you.*

That point may sound like little more than common sense to you, but I highlight it because it's not always common practice. When we want to affect the way our teenagers think, for example, do we first step back and consider what they'd truly find compelling? Do we take the time to consider what's important to them? What their fears are? What their needs and desires are? How they view the world? Or do we just take the expedient route of defaulting to the way we've always tried to shape their attitudes and behaviors? If we do the latter, it might explain why things are not working.

This same lesson applies in the workplace. With your boss, for instance, the more you can get into his or her head and understand his or her constraints and pressures and ego, the more likely you are to generate ideas and solutions that your boss will embrace. With your customers, as well, and your employees, before you say a word, stand in their shoes and view the situation from that vantage point. Remember, people do things for their reasons, not yours.

Stand in their shoes and view the situation from that vantage point. Remember, people do things for their reasons, not yours.

This is a universal principle, so consider it in whatever context is most relevant to you—the workplace, the home, the mission field, wherever. Are you really in the habit of taking the time to know your audience? Do your persuasion attempts begin with a thorough understanding of the person or people you're trying to influence? And if you do make this attempt, *are you sure you've really understood*?

Try not to gloss over this latter question. Address it in humility, since the consequences of overconfidence can be substantial. Pastors, for example, often assume they know their congregation, and they design their sermons and their programs based on this assumption. But according to one nationwide study, they may be way off base. Pastors in that survey say that 70 percent of their "congregants deem their faith in God to be the highest priority in their life." But when the researchers asked those in the pews, only *15 percent* said their faith was their highest priority![1]

Think of the implications here. Think about how many pastors are missing the mark with their messages and their whole discipleship programs because they misunderstand their audience. And—here's the crux of the matter—think about how many more lives would be affected and how much more influence our churches would have if pastors and other church leaders knew their flock better.

How Paul Used This Principle in Athens

As you see, "knowing your audience" is an indispensable step in the influence process. It's essential to learn as much as possible about the people we're trying to persuade.

The apostle Paul certainly did. He was exceptional at this. For example, do you remember the scene at Mars Hill (Acts 17)? There's Paul, toe-to-toe with a gaggle of gabby Greek gurus. These people spend all their time just sitting around and debating the fashionable ideas of the day. Sizing up Paul, they're laughing at this little man, at least privately. Small in stature and seemingly even smaller in intellect, what could he possibly teach *them*?

But Paul has anticipated this. Pulling from his quiver the "know your audience" principle, Paul plans his influence around how these guys think. He knows their cultural hubris, he knows their assumption of ethnic and cerebral superiority, and he knows their thirst for knowledge. Armed with all this information, *Paul starts where they are.* He steps to their side, so to speak and begins with their assumption about the legitimacy and accuracy of their worldview. Brilliantly, as we see from these verses, he argues from within their worldview:

> Men of Athens, I see that you are extremely religious in every respect. For as I was passing through and observing the objects of your worship, I even found an altar on which was inscribed: TO AN UNKNOWN GOD. Therefore, what you worship in ignorance, this I proclaim to you. (Acts 17:22–23)

Can you see what Paul is doing here? Do you see the subtle genius in his method? Paul is arguing not from his own understanding of the world but from theirs, starting with their "unknown god." He's fitting his message into their mind-set, rather than immediately challenging their beliefs. As a result, they're staying with him instead of walking away or mentally formulating their rebuttals.

Paul starts where they are. He steps to their side, so to speak, and argues from within their worldview.

Then, to this group that values intellectual growth so much, he hits the bull's-eye. He tells them, in essence, I'm going to help you learn even more: "what you worship in

principle. What situations were they dealing with? How did those people show that they knew their audience?

Think about the greatest influence challenge or challenges in your life. What do you need to know about this person or these people before you choose an influence strategy? Make some notes about personality traits, values, beliefs, background, or other factors that would be helpful in understanding that person or persons.

PART 2

Lay a Foundation of Relationship and Respect

Missionaries, parents, teachers, pastors, salespeople—all have one thing in common. At least the successful ones do. They take the time to build relationships with the people they seek to influence. Relationship culminates in trust, which culminates in earning the right to be heard on important issues. As a result, influence happens more naturally in the context of a relationship than it does with strangers.

Having said that, it's important to remind ourselves that it's easy to misuse these influence principles. In this case, misuse would mean to develop relationships with people for the sole purpose of persuading them of something. Not a good idea. Certainly not a Christian idea. But as the next three principles will show, Jesus used relationship building with a pure heart and with godly motives. We should faithfully follow his lead.

These three principles we see in action almost every day—principles that we ourselves use often. The approaches of *connecting through similarity, serving people's needs,* and *asking for the other person's opinion* are fundamental. Our tasks in Part 2 of this book are to understand these methods through a scriptural lens, to solidify our understanding by applying them to our personal influence opportunities, and to recognize how to use them exclusively in ways that honor God.

— PRINCIPLE 4 —

Connect through Similarity

There's an old story that I heard a few times growing up in and around various churches, but I never understood its power until recently. It goes something like this:

It was Christmas Eve, and the Jones family was heading to church—everyone except Dad, that is. Dad had little use for churches; he thought they were full of hypocrites, and besides, that "God becoming man" story was simply too bizarre to be believable. So he had stopped attending years ago.

This particular Christmas Eve was an especially easy decision for him. It was snowing. A lot. He even tried to talk his wife out of lugging the kids through the storm. But they went anyway as he curled up by the fire with his remote.

A few minutes after they left, the man heard a noise at the bay window. A small bird was trying to get in the house to escape the snow. The man watched with uncharacteristic empathy as the bird fluttered desperately from pane to pane, attracted by the light inside.

The man went out to see if he could help. He knew there wasn't much he could do, but he did have a shed nearby. Maybe, he thought, I can shoo the bird into the shed to ride out the storm.

Well, as you can imagine, his attempt was almost comical. Every time the man came near, the bird just flew to another window and continued its futile attempt to escape the elements. Eventually, snow started to accumulate on its head and body.

The man—more of a snowman by this point—made one last attempt to chase the bird to safety, but it was hopeless. Birds don't understand people. They're afraid of people. They flee from them, and that's just what this bird did. Then a strange, seemingly nonsensical thought came to the man: if only I were a bird, even for one minute, I could lead this bird to the safety of the shed.

If only I were a bird. Silly thought, but then again, maybe it wasn't. In fact, maybe it was a divinely-planted thought. You see, at that very moment it dawned on the man why God may have taken on human flesh. Maybe God, too, wanted to lead us out of danger, and maybe the best way to do that was for God to become like us.

The Power of Similarity

Cute little story, isn't it? The lesson's not so little, though. It's this: *Similarity opens the door to influence.* It encourages people (or birds, for that matter) to follow when they might not otherwise do so.

Think about it. Isn't it the case that we're more receptive to the ideas of those who are like us in many ways? Don't we listen more closely to people who have the same set of spiritual or political beliefs? When going through a tough time, isn't it someone who's walked through that same trial who can comfort us the most? At work, isn't our opinion of our company shaped more by our coworkers' opinions than by managers two or three levels up? At the department store, don't we see women selling cosmetics to women? On TV, don't we see seventy-year-olds selling low-cost life insurance to senior citizens?

This influence-through-similarity principle is everywhere, even in our churches. I know a youth pastor—a guy in his *mid-forties*, mind you—who has an incredible influence on teens. It might feel a little weird for me to hang out with him, though, since his hair is bleached and spiked, he occasionally wears a nose ring, he talks incessantly about the up-and-coming rock bands, and he's a video game junky. Don't get me wrong—he's a sold-out Christian and a mature believer, and his messages to the kids are solid truth. But to look at him is cognitive dissonance: forty-five going on sixteen.

Similarity breeds relationship, relationship breeds trust, and trust ultimately breeds influence.

That's just the point, though. His similarity with the teens—his looks, his musical taste, his jewelry, his prowess with the PlayStation, even the way he speaks—has built a bridge that spans the generation gap. It's a bridge called "relationship," and it leads to a land called "trust." He shapes these kids' attitudes and behaviors like no other adult can, not even their parents.

Do you see the progression here? For this youth pastor, similarity breeds relationship, relationship breeds trust, and trust ultimately breeds influence.

The same thing happens with missionaries. Those who minister overseas learn the customs and language of their target people or group before ever setting foot on foreign soil. The best way to establish the relationship necessary to credibly share the gospel is to be similar to those they're trying to reach. This is also why, after some in that target group have converted to the Christian faith, the missionary asks these new converts to take the lead in evangelism. It's just more effective. People are persuaded by similar people more than they are by dissimilar people, and the greater the similarity, the greater the likelihood of persuasion.

The incarnation is perhaps the best example of the similarity principle in action. Jesus looked no different from those of his day, wore similar clothing, lived like they did, ate what they ate, and drank what they drank.

I believe this is why God took on human flesh and walked among us for three decades. And I believe further that this is why Jesus looked no different from those of his day, wore similar clothing, lived like they did, ate what they ate, and drank what they drank. He was different from them in many respects, for sure, but similar in enough ways to lead them (and now us) out of the winter storm.

Paul's Use of the Similarity Principle

Let's look at another biblical example to solidify our understanding of this principle. Paul loved to use the similarity principle. He even says so, boldly and directly:

For although I am free from all people, I have made myself a slave to all, in order to win more people. To the Jews I became like a Jew, to win Jews; to those under the law, like one under the law—though I myself am not under the law—to win those under the law. To those who are outside the law, like one outside the law—not being outside God's law, but under the law of Christ—to win those outside the law. To the weak I became weak,

in order to win the weak. I have become all things
to all people, so that I may by all means save some.
(1 Cor. 9:19–22)

This is not compromise or inconsistency, but the
shrewd practice of adaptation. Paul wasn't in the habit of
using canned, off-the-shelf messages like so many of our
speakers today because he cared about real influence, real
change, and real transformation of hearts. That usually
requires starting on common ground, so he adapted his
communications and style to emphasize similarities with
his audience. He even adapted his name, changing it from
Saul (a Hebrew name) to Paul (the Roman form of Saul),
to be more effective in the Gentile world.

This approach also saved his neck on a few occasions. Consider back-to-back incidents described in the
book of Acts, interactions with the Romans and then the
Sanhedrin. If you know Paul, you know he has some commonality with both of these groups, so you might even be
able to predict what he's going to do. He's in hot water with
each group in Acts 22 and 23, and he needs to think fast to
avoid getting boiled.

First, he has to influence the Roman soldiers. Paul is
being chased, hunted actually, by a mob of Jews who want
him dead for allegedly teaching Jews to abandon Mosaic
Law. Roman soldiers snatch Paul from the crowd but then
plan to beat him ruthlessly for causing the riot. In the nick
of time, Paul whips out the similarity principle, asking the
guard: "Is it legal for you to scourge a man who is a Roman
citizen and is uncondemned?" (Acts 22:25).

You're a Roman citizen? the commander asks incredu-
lously. *A man similar to us? A man with the same rights we
have?* When Paul confirms this and adds that he was even
born a citizen, rather than paying his way into the club, the
Romans back off instantly.

They don't rough him up, but they don't set him free, either. Instead, the Romans bring Paul before the Sanhedrin—the seventy-member supreme counsel of Judaism—to fully investigate the charges. Now he's *really* in trouble because the Sanhedrin is predisposed to find Paul guilty, and they have the power to impose capital punishment.

But watch this. It's probably Paul's most clever use of the similarity principle to influence a situation:

> When Paul realized that one part of them were Sadducees and the other part were Pharisees, he cried out in the Sanhedrin, "Brothers, I am a Pharisee, a son of Pharisees! I am being judged because of the hope of the resurrection of the dead!"
>
> When he said this, a dispute broke out between the Pharisees and the Sadducees, and the assembly was divided. For the Sadducees say there is no resurrection, and no angel or spirit, but the Pharisees affirm them all.
>
> The shouting grew loud, and some of the scribes of the Pharisees' party got up and argued vehemently: "We find nothing evil in this man. What if a spirit or an angel has spoken to him?" When the dispute became violent, the commander feared that Paul might be torn apart by them and ordered the troops to go down, rescue him from them, and bring him into the barracks. (Acts 23:6–10)

Paul doesn't misrepresent himself. He doesn't even defend himself. He just identifies a commonality with one group, and that's enough to rescue him from the potentially lethal situation.

Brilliant move, wasn't it? Paul quickly takes off his Roman citizen hat and replaces it with his dusty old Pharisee hat, seating himself firmly on one side of the aisle. In doing so, he exploits a major wedge issue that separated the two factions in the Sanhedrin—resurrection—thereby getting the body to fight with itself rather than with him.

Talk about the power of knowing your audience (Principle 3)! And talk about connecting through similarity (Principle 4)! Paul's slick here, plain and simple, and it works beautifully. He doesn't misrepresent himself. He doesn't even defend himself. He just identifies a commonality with one group and that's enough to rescue him from the potentially lethal situation.

A Long-Term Approach

Now you may never find yourself in such a dire situation, but rest assured that this principle of influence operates just as effectively when your life is not on the line. To gain more influence with your boss, your spouse, your kids, your neighbors, your friends, your parents, complete strangers, or anyone else, identify similarities and work from there. Sometimes this is easy because there are obvious points of intersection; other times it will require *developing* those commonalities—like doing more things *with* your kids rather than just *for* your kids. Remember the youth pastor.

That doesn't mean you need to dye your hair or pierce your nose, but it does mean committing to a relationship-building approach to influence where payoff is not immediate. It might entail coaching your child's ball team or taking cooking classes with your mate or finally getting to know your employees and your neighbors—things we should arguably be doing anyway as Christians. In doing so, you'll develop the common ground necessary to eventually lead them where God wants them to go.

For Reflection

Principle 4, the "connect through similarity" principle, says that we're more easily persuaded by people similar to us than by those who are different. Where have you seen this principle in operation? Jot down some situations in your notebook or journal.

Think about the greatest influence challenge or challenges in your life. Ask yourself these questions: What do I have in common with the person or persons I want to influence that could be a starting point for relationship and discussion? Are we of similar ages; cultural, social, or ethnic backgrounds; educational levels; careers? Are we parents, students, members of a club or group?

Or should I instead work through others who are more similar to the person I'm trying to influence? Who might be a good influencer in this person's life?

—PRINCIPLE 5 —

Serve Their Needs

A lot of times, the people I'm dealing with are extremely nasty. . . . To diffuse the situation, I've got to try to understand what's in his head. The first step to getting there is to show him some respect, which shows my sincerity and reliability. So before the bad guy demands anything, I always ask him if he needs something.

Obviously, I'm not going to give him a car. I'm not going to let him go. But it makes excellent sense to be sensitive to the other guy's needs. When you give somebody a little something, he feels obligated to give you something back. That's just common sense.

—Hostage Negotiator Dominick Misino,
New York Police Department[1]

Be sensitive to the other guy's needs" and then "give him a little something." If it works with people who are "extremely nasty," it will work with the significantly nicer people you're trying to influence, too.

As you can also see from Mr. Misino's comment, this principle of influence builds off a previous one. Unless you "know your audience" (Principle 3), you'd be hard pressed to give the other person something he or she values. When you do, though, the universally-recognized law of reciprocity kicks in: you're likely to receive back the very behavior you offer. Even a hostage-taker "feels obligated to give you something back."

In Christianese, we'd say, "For whatever a man sows he will also reap" (Gal. 6:7). And just look at the reciprocal effects Jesus teaches:

> Do not judge, and you will not be judged. Do
> not condemn, and you will not be condemned.
> Forgive, and you will be forgiven. Give, and it will
> be given to you. . . . For with the measure you use,
> it will be measured back to you. (Luke 6:37–38)

You'll get back what you give, Jesus and Paul told their audiences. Now, two millennia later, though much has changed, what influences people's behavior hasn't. We still tend to return the very behavior we receive from people. We reciprocate, for better or worse.

On the down side, this means that a raised voice begets a raised voice, escalating the argument. Road rage sparks counter-rage, landing people in the hospital. Insults are repaid in kind, poisoning relationships. Broken promises yield more of the same, destroying trust.

At the same time forgiveness begets forgiveness, and relationships are mended. Listening to them causes them to listen to you, and understanding breaks through. Your concession prompts their concession, and deals are made. Kindness engenders kindness, and friendships are born.

This is probably the influence principle
that is more easily abused than any other.

This is good news for us would-be influencers. In many situations, and quite powerfully in situations where a relationship is strained or even hostile, you'll find that influence begins by modeling the very behavior you want to receive. You can think of it, perhaps, as the Golden Rule of Influence.

But let's be careful about this and perfectly clear: this is probably the influence principle that is more easily abused than any other. *We Christians cannot and should not be in the business of serving people just to get something back from them.* Ours is a worldview that stresses service to others out of love for God, not as a tactic to secure their compliance. So as we consider the influence implications of reaping and sowing, we need to do so with a commitment to using this principle with a pure heart and for God's purposes.

Influence through Serving People's Needs

Here are two examples of the biblical nature and practice of this principle. The first is a concept that you may have seen before; the second is one you probably haven't.

First consider "servant leadership." Ever hear the term? It's used increasingly to describe a biblically consistent approach that Christians could take in leading others, whether at work, in the home, in the church, in Congress, or anywhere else. Jesus himself teaches the paradigm as he reveals to his disciples the nature of God-honoring leadership:

> You know that the rulers of the Gentiles dominate them, and the men of high position exercise power over them. It must not be like that among you. On the contrary, whoever wants to become great among you must be your servant, and whoever wants to be first among you must be your slave; just as the Son of Man did not come to be served, but to serve, and to give His life—a ransom for many. (Matt. 20:25–28)

Now try that at GE or GM or just about any organization, for that matter. It sounds more like the stay-at-home moms I know than the CEOs I know.

How about you? Have you ever seen authentic servant leadership in action? Have you ever been around someone who seems to care more about your needs than his or her needs? A person who truly delights in serving God by serving you? If you've been blessed with this unusually happy experience, then I'd guess that you'd do almost anything for that person. He or she could make some pretty enormous requests of you, and you'd say yes, right? That's because the biblical axiom remains true: sow service, reap service. Sow kindness, reap kindness. Sow love, reap love. It's not rocket science, but it's every bit as powerful.

One of the reasons Jesus had so many people following him is that he was a leader who served selflessly.

Service and sacrifice lay the groundwork for the best kind of influence. And yes, the principle can be easily abused—you can choose to serve someone simply as a manipulation tactic. When it's misused, though, it's not the principle that's at fault; it's the (mis)user.

To avoid that, make a habit of looking to the One who modeled the proper practice of this principle. One of the reasons Jesus had such tremendous influence over people while he was on the earth, and why he had so many people following him, is that he was a leader who served selflessly. His ministry was one of healing others, feeding others, teaching others, giving others hope for eternity that they never had before. Others, others, others. Who wouldn't follow such a person? Who can resist saying yes to someone who is the embodiment of compassion?

We can't, at least not when we truly grasp Jesus' compassion for us. Do you recall the last time you really felt the depth of this love? Let me help you remember: the revelation generates some tears and a fervent willingness to do anything for him, even surrender our stubborn will to live as he wants us to live. That's how influence through service works.

Nehemiah's Genius

The second example comes from the Old Testament book of Nehemiah, the story of a man whose actions show us that serving others' needs does more than build a bank account of good will. Service is also a powerful ally to get things done that God wants done.

Nehemiah was a descendant of the Jewish population that had been taken captive by the Babylonians. The Jewish exiles were eventually permitted to return home to Jerusalem, though their city was in ruins. Decades later Nehemiah, who was at that point a cupbearer for the Persian king (i.e., the person who tasted the king's food and drink to protect the king from being poisoned), learned that Jerusalem still was in a deplorable condition, vulnerable to outside attack because its city walls had not been rebuilt. So Nehemiah asked his boss for a sabbatical to oversee the rebuilding himself.

After receiving royal permission, Nehemiah went to work, organizing a labor force, securing materials, and dealing with multiple enemies of the rebuilding project—a project slated for completion in fewer than two months.

Now consider the challenge: get the wall built fast and at the same time make sure it's of the highest quality. Sound familiar to those of you who have worked a few years? We're often put in this conundrum with no option to trade efficiency for effectiveness. But Nehemiah got it done. How? By leveraging the very principle we're talking about here: he started by thinking about the needs of the workers who would be building the wall.

Nehemiah got the wall rebuilt fast and right by identifying and serving people's needs.

Consider this. It's exceedingly clever. To get the work done fast and right, *Nehemiah had each person rebuild the part of the wall that was closest to that person's house* (Neh. 3). Think about that for a minute. Is that brilliant or what? He wants to get the wall rebuilt in a way that guarantees its quality since if any portion of the wall is weak, the whole city is vulnerable. But the management problem from the beginning of time has been getting workers to care about what the boss cares about. Nehemiah ingeniously solves this problem by identifying the workers' most pressing need—*the security of their own houses*—and then assigning tasks in a way that meets that need. By designing the task to serve the workers' own self-interest, that is, by having each person rebuild the part of the wall that was closest to his house, this general contractor influenced his team to engage in exactly the right behaviors, yielding top quality in a timely manner. He got the job done by identifying and serving people's needs.

Now perhaps you're one of those people who don't see this as all that clever. Perhaps it seems obvious to you that this should have been Nehemiah's approach. Two comments about that. First, remember that I told you that influence through serving needs isn't rocket science. When we fail at this, it's usually because we forget to do it or we're too stubborn to do it. And second, if you think Nehemiah's decision was an obvious choice, then that's great news for you; you already have the instincts necessary to put this principle into practice. You may have been doing so for years already. That's a grace you shouldn't take for granted and one that you should continue to share with everyone God's entrusted to you.

Use This Principle Everywhere

There are dozens of applications of this principle, well beyond hostage negotiations, servant leadership, and project management. In marriage, for example, keeping foremost on your mind the service question, What does my mate want, and how can I exceed that? will move the two of you toward the mutually-influential relationship God wants you to have. In parenting, meeting your kids' psychological and spiritual needs (not just their physical needs) will give you greater influence at every stage of their development. And in evangelism, service and sacrifice for others earn you the right to be heard where it matters the most.

It's easy to misuse this principle by serving for pragmatic reasons alone. God has a better plan for you, though. Serve others to serve him. Then he will return the blessing to you many times over.

For Reflection

The "serve their needs" principle says that meeting people's needs and desires makes them more receptive to our requests. Where have you seen this principle in operation? Jot down some people you've observed who are particularly adept at putting this principle into practice.

Think about the greatest influence challenge or challenges in your life. Ask yourself, what does this person value that I could give to him or her? What actions can I take to give that person what he or she thinks is important or essential?

Ask for Their Opinion

My friend Mike is really smart, one of the smartest guys I know, in fact. He earned a 4.0 at every school he ever attended all the way through grad school. Mike's got a lot of creativity, as well. For example, when he wanted to get his nine- and seven-year-old boys interested in the book of Proverbs, he knew that a straight devotional approach would fall flat. The proverb-a-day calendar seemed hokey, and he couldn't find a decent kid-friendly resource that would do the job. So he made up his own approach to teaching them Solomon's wisdom, calling their nightly lessons "Learning from the Wise Guy." Is that clever, or what? The idea was an instant hit with the kids, and it remains a family tradition to this day.

Mike recently told me about another of his innovations that happens to be right on point in regard to Principle 6. He's got good kids, but cleaning up their room is not high on their list of priorities (no matter what the "wise guy" says). So the last time they balked at cleaning, Mike whipped up this little gem. Maybe you've used it, as well. Mike just started cleaning their room himself, while the kids looked on dumbfounded. Dad just didn't do that sort of thing.

After about sixty seconds, Mike started asking the boys questions: Where does this go? What's this thing for? Do you know if these two things go together?

You probably know what's coming. The boys, now consultants rather than indentured servants, jumped at the chance to teach their dad something. It's hard to resist giving answers when we know them. And within another minute, they were doing more than consulting; they were actually doing the cleaning themselves, first alongside Dad, and eventually by themselves. No yelling. No threats. No bribery. Just questions—patient, respectful questions.

What Mike did in the most subtle of ways to influence his boys we can do every day if we'll be patient and charitable enough to do it. Seeking the opinion of the person you're trying to influence is among the shrewdest of persuasion principles because it builds on a fundamental pillar of human nature: the desire to have our opinion respected. We all think of ourselves as reasonably smart, right? Most of us think that we have good answers to the problems we see around us. And almost everyone likes to be asked for his or her ideas. Mix together those ingredients, toss the concoction in the oven, and out pops this axiom: *When people are asked for their opinion, they want to offer it.*

Think that's a pretty bland cake? Wait a few paragraphs for the aftertaste. "Asking their opinion" is not just some trick-your-gullible-kid influence principle. And it's not just some jujitsu-like tactic to leverage people's pride to your advantage. As we learn from Jesus himself, "asking their opinion" is nothing less than a biblically-based lesson that we can apply in almost any influence situation.

How Jesus Used This Principle, Part 1

On more than one occasion, Jesus used this approach to influence. Consider his interaction with a legal expert, as Luke tells it (Luke 10:25–28):

> Just then an expert in the law stood up to test Him, saying, "Teacher, what must I do to inherit eternal life?"
>
> "What is written in the law?" [Jesus] asked him. "How do you read it?"
>
> He answered: "Love the Lord your God with all your heart, with all your soul, with all your strength, and with all your mind; and your neighbor as yourself."
>
> "You've answered correctly," He told him. "Do this and you will live."

Set aside for the moment that this guy's being disingenuous in asking the question—that he's standing up to test Jesus. Regardless of the man's intentions, Jesus treats this as a teachable moment. He knows the guy's smart, and he knows that the guy's not exactly predisposed to be influenced. So what does Jesus do in response to the question? Well, what he *doesn't* do is give an immediate answer. The expert in the law is expecting that and is likely armed with a briefcase full of retorts to whatever Jesus would say. Rather, Jesus uses a consultative approach to influence, asking the man what he thinks.

Jesus treats this as a teachable moment. But rather than giving an answer, Jesus uses a consultative approach to influence, asking the man what he thinks.

Don't miss this. It's Jesus' power tool for dealing with smart people and skeptics alike, and he's giving us a tutorial in how to use it here.

When Jesus asks him for his perspective, the expert in the law responds with what we call today the Great Commandment. No one could give a better answer, right?

And because of that, Jesus affirms the insightful response, thereby disarming the man. The lawyer was picking a fight, but he picked off an olive branch instead.

The man apparently doesn't like that too much. He still is "wanting to justify himself," so, stroking his beard, he fires back a lawyerly follow-up question: "And who is my neighbor?" (Luke 10:29). Regardless of the nefarious motivation, it still seems like a fair question. Define your terms, Master.

Again Jesus turns this around by asking the man's opinion, but cleverly he does so in the context of a story, Jesus' primary pathway to persuasion (which I will discuss in the next chapter, Principle 7). To answer the "neighbor" question, Jesus relates the stunning parable of the Good Samaritan and then, most germane for our purposes here, tosses the question back to the lawyer: "Which of these three do you think proved to be a neighbor to the man who fell into the hands of robbers?" (v. 36).

The answer's obvious, and the lawyer gets it right again: "The one who had mercy on him" (v. 37). Then and only then, *after asking the man's opinion*, does Jesus provide his answer: You're right, the Samaritan. Now "go and do the same" (v. 37).

I don't know if the expert walked away persuaded of anything. Scripture doesn't tell us. But it's Jesus' process that we're examining right now, not the outcome. It reveals a truth we don't often think about, much less implement: *Sometimes the best answer is not to answer, at least not right away.* Ask for the other person's perspective first, and then build your conversation from there.

A word of caution, though: when you do ask for the other person's perspective, be careful to avoid the common mistakes of a snide tone or confrontational nonverbal cues, despite how you might feel. Such things torpedo the whole approach (imagine Jesus asking the lawyer's opinion using a condescending tone, for example). Instead, try to ask in an unemotional and even humble manner. Let your question be genuine, and let your listening be charitable. You may be surprised by the results.

Remember, the smarter someone thinks he or she is, the more important this technique becomes. It's also an approach that you can use in many other situations, too, and in particular, situations where you want to encourage someone *to really think* about an issue, rather than just passively listening. Let me show you how Jesus did this as well.

How Jesus Used This Principle, Part 2

Place yourself in the setting for a moment, even if you've heard this sequence of stories from Luke 9 a thousand times (and perhaps *especially* if you've heard it a thousand times). Imagine you're among the group of twelve disciples that has just returned from the mission field. Jesus sent them out; now they're back. There's an excitement and energy in this group like they've never experienced. Over the past several days, they found themselves speaking eloquent words, prophetic words, *life-changing words*, just as they had heard their Master speak.

Though they had always been powerless, suddenly they could just lay hands on someone and by speaking the name of Jesus, heal that person! Bartholomew raves about curing a blind man. Peter one-ups him saying he cured two. Thomas trumps them all, telling of how he cleansed a leper with a mere touch of his pinky. A few of them, with eyes wide, slowly back away from Thomas.

Jesus is smiling, rejoicing with them. But his joy is noticeably tempered. He needs to show them the reality, to deflate their puff and connect them to the larger picture. He does it not with an answer but with a question, not by telling them directly but by asking their opinion.

He first asks them an easy question: "Who do people say that I am?" Their responses come so fast that they interrupt one another: *Some called you Elijah, and some think you're John the Baptist. Others just say you're one of the prophets from long ago, back from the dead. Two guys in Cana actually got in a shouting match over which prophet you are!*

Are you there with the group? Can you feel their exuberance? Are you close enough to sense the subtle arrogance in their answers? Are you perhaps even shaking your head with them at the misguided ideas that some people had about Jesus? I have to admit, I might have been, had I been among them. He's Elijah? He's John the Baptist? Give me a break!

But then Jesus asks the real question on his mind, the question designed to get them to *think*, the question designed to influence them once and for all by publicly putting them on the record. He asks for their opinion: "And who do *you* say that I am?"

The chuckling quickly subsides. Smiles morph to seriousness. Soon, only the crackling fire is audible, as each man glances at Jesus and then breaks eye contact, lest he be called on to respond.

By asking for their opinion, Jesus' question involves them, wrenching them from their comfort zone and compelling them to finally deal with the issue for themselves.

The silence lasts long enough for each disciple to answer the question privately, in his own heart. It becomes a persuasive moment because it's an interactive moment. By asking for their opinion, Jesus' question involves them, wrenching them from their comfort zone of judging the folly of others, and compelling them finally to deal with the issue for themselves.

It's easy to poke fun at others' ideas. It softens a person's edge, though, when *he or she* is called on to offer better ideas. This is another reason a consultative posture can be so influential. Not only does it respect the other person, as we said, but it also causes that person to participate actively in the conversation and in the problem solving—a deeper level of thinking that potentially paves the way for a new understanding.

Who is this man called Jesus? Suddenly, when Jesus asks for the disciples' opinion, it's not just everyone else's problem to solve; it's their problem, too. And their collective answer, eventually voiced through Peter—"God's Messiah!"—influences them profoundly, escalating their commitment to follow.

An Ancient Approach, a Contemporary Application

You might be interested to know that this approach to influence—asking for opinions before giving answers—is alive and well today, increasingly popular among professional and amateur evangelists alike. According to a nationwide survey by the Barna Research Group, of those who have invited someone to consider the Christian faith within the past twelve months, a significant majority did so through the soft, nonthreatening approach of asking questions. To quote the findings:

> Another popular approach was to "start a discussion with a non-Christian in which you intentionally asked what they believe concerning a particular moral or spiritual matter, and continued to ask questions about their views without telling them they are wrong, but continuing to nicely

challenge them to explain their thinking and its implications." Known as "Socratic evangelism" because of its dialogical nature, seven out of ten believers (69 percent) said they had engaged in this approach.[1]

"Socratic evangelism." Pretty smart, if you ask me. It's respectful, it keeps the conversation going, it takes the onus off of us, and it encourages serious consideration by the other side. What more could you ask for? Come to think of it, "Socratic parenting" might not be a bad idea in some situations. Or "Socratic preaching." Or "Socratic leadership." Or in your case, Socratic _____.

Let me ask your opinion about something: How well do you think that would work?

For Reflection

Principle 6, "Ask for their opinion," says that people are more likely to be persuaded if they're part of the process. Where have you seen this principle in operation?

Jot down in your journal where you have seen it being used, along with the name or description of the person who used it. Was it a preacher? A teacher? An employer? A politician? A parent talking to a child? A customer service representative? Someone else?

Think about the greatest influence challenge or challenges in your life. Ask yourself, have I asked for this person's solutions and ideas, and have I genuinely listened to him or her?

PART 3

Reframe
the Situation

I love all the principles of influence Jesus modeled, but the three in this section are among my favorites because they're so subtle. They can influence people without their ever knowing that they're being influenced.

I don't mean that in a subversive, manipulative way, of course. I simply mean that what they exemplify is "invisible influence." The approaches of *storytelling*, *contrast*, and *metaphor* are indirect pathways to persuasion, and in many situations that's exactly what's required.

Jesus modeled each one of these approaches for us. He was a master storyteller, regaling people throughout the countryside with parable after parable—stories that entertained while they educated. Before those in the crowd knew it, they were face-to-face with a life-changing truth, and they retained that truth because it was easy to remember the story from which it came.

Jesus also creatively used the approaches of contrast and metaphor to help people see timeless truths in new ways. By changing their frame of reference, Jesus changed people's thinking and behavior—again, not with a formal argument or direct evidence and not with openly telling them to change, but merely with subtle, ingenious word choices, sometimes totaling no more than two or three words.

Ingenious, indeed. But as you'll see, we don't need to be geniuses to follow Jesus' example. In fact, most of us use each of these techniques at least once in awhile. To follow Jesus' lead more faithfully, we simply need to understand these three influence principles a little better, to fine-tune our skills with them, and to be more intentional in planning to use them.

These are some of the most powerful concepts among the fifteen in this book, so continue to look for their application to your most pressing influence challenges.

Tell a Story

Since we're covering the principle of storytelling, what better way to start than with a story? This is a true one.

I have an eleven-year-old son who is half Irish and half Italian. Pity the poor boy; his hardwiring has yielded many wonderful attributes but also a temper that epitomizes the stereotypes of those two fabulous cultures. Like his father, he's had to learn a thing or two about releasing one's anger in an appropriate manner. I've done everything I can think of to help him in this regard, including trying to model the appropriate behaviors (Principle 2), educating myself about kids' emotions (Principle 3), relationship building through similar interests (Principle 4), seeking his solutions (Principle 6), showing him relevant passages in books like Proverbs and James (Principle 10), and administering a plethora of time-outs and other consequences (Principle 14). That's just a sampling, by the way; I've tried a few other things, as well. And to be honest, each of these methods has produced some positive results. But not one of them ever had the effect of reading him a story from Bill Bennett's *A Children's Book of Virtues*.

In that book is a story about Genghis Khan, a Mongolian warlord from the thirteenth century who was known for, among other things, his blistering temper. Khan was hunting with his pet hawk, a trusted friend who helped him find game to shoot. He was alone in the woods and very thirsty but had no water with him, so when he came across some water dripping slowly from a rock ledge, he was elated. Khan took a cup and, over the course of a couple minutes, filled it drop by drop. But just as he tried to drink the water, his pet hawk swooped down and knocked the cup from his hand, spilling the water on the ground. This was strange and unprecedented behavior for the hawk.

Khan was enraged and returned his cup to the ledge, waiting a couple more minutes for it to refill. Again, just as he was about to drink it, the hawk knocked the drink from his hand. Khan screamed at the hawk, warning him that if he did it again, he'd be dead. And sure enough, minutes later, when the hawk again prevented Khan from taking a drink, Khan struck down the bird with his sword.

By now, the water had stopped dripping, so an infuriated Khan had to scale the rock ledge to find where the water had come from. When he reached the top he found a lake—with an enormous (think "sea monster"), poisonous snake lying dead in it. The snake's body blocked the path of the water that had been dripping down the rock ledge, and immediately, Khan realized that the water he intended to drink was venomous. His pet hawk, having seen the snake from above, had saved his life, but Khan's uncontrolled anger caused him to repay the heroic bird with death.

My son, an animal lover, sat in stunned horror, transfixed by the picture of this poor, dying bird at the feet of a sword-wielding soldier. Tears filled Michael's eyes (an unusual event). He couldn't sleep for hours that night. The story triggered a flood of emotions—and, I think, a flood of revelation—that no punishment, no Bible verse, no parental relationship ever had. Through the story and the picture, he *felt* for the first time the destructive power of improperly released anger, and it had a profound effect on him for a long time.

That's not to say that he (or his dad) no longer struggles with the issue. It is to say, though, that the emotional appeal of a story, coupled with the graphic picture of the consequences of unmanaged anger, affected him more than any other influence method.

The Influence Method Most Likely to Change Behavior

Aside from prayer, storytelling, especially when it tugs at the emotions of another person, is the influence principle that is most likely to get your listeners to actually *do* something—to change their behavior. I recognize that's an audacious statement, considering the enormous power of the other principles. But it seems a little less audacious when we consider that storytelling was Jesus' primary means of teaching and influencing others.

> Aside from prayer, storytelling, especially when it tugs at the emotions of another person, is the influence principle that is most likely to get your listeners to actually *do* something.

When we think of Jesus' teachings, we think of stories, don't we? Parables. Lessons taught through familiar experiences, at least familiar to the original hearers—farming, weddings, employment, borrowing and lending, tending sheep. They were really just an extension of what we now call the "oral tradition." Due to the scarcity of both writing implements and literacy, every ancient culture passed along its wisdom and tradition orally and anecdotally. In doing so, it influenced the next generation to embrace long-standing values.

Jesus used stories for far more than this, though. Rather than just perpetuating values of old, he introduced through parable an entirely different way of relating to God and neighbor. To teach that God's forgiveness is always available, no matter what we've done, he told the Prodigal Son story. To teach that it's never too late to be saved, he told the Workers in the Vineyard story. To teach us how to pray and how not to pray, he told the parable of the Tax Collector and the Pharisee. To teach that we are to love and serve all people, regardless of who they are or how busy we are, he told the Good Samaritan story.

In this way, he influenced thousands of his contemporaries and billions since then to see differently. How does this work? It's not just that Jesus' stories offered clever analogies to everyday experience or that they were simply memorable tales. A major reason is that Jesus' stories, like all of the most influential stories throughout history, *touched people's emotions*. They had "pathos," to borrow Aristotle's term for the influence principle—the power to evoke feelings and arouse emotions.

> Jesus introduced through parable
> an entirely different way of relating
> to God and neighbor.

Consider for a moment the parable of the Good Samaritan. Nice story about a couple big-wigs whose heads were too big for their wig, right? And about a little guy who did a big thing, right? Wrong. If we hear the story through the ears of the original Jewish audience, it's not nearly that tepid. It's a completely scandalous story. Because the protagonist is a Samaritan—essentially an impure, half-Jew—few stories could be more offensive. In fact, according to renowned seminary professors

Gordon Fee and Douglas Stuart, if Jesus told the parable today, it would sound something like this:

> A family of disheveled, unkempt individuals was stranded by the side of the road on a Sunday morning. They were in obvious distress. The mother was sitting on a tattered suitcase, hair uncombed, clothes in disarray, with a glazed look to her eyes, holding a smelly, poorly-clad, crying baby. The father was unshaved, dressed in coveralls, the look of despair as he tried to corral two other youngsters. Beside them was a run-down old car that had obviously just given up the ghost.
>
> Down the road came a car driven by the local bishop; he was on his way to church. And though the father of the family waved frantically, the bishop could not hold up his parishioners, so he acted as if he didn't see them.
>
> Soon came another car, and again the father waved furiously. But the car was driven by the president of the local Kiwanis Club, and he was late for a statewide meeting of Kiwanis presidents in a nearby city. He too acted as if he did not see them, and kept his eyes straight on the road ahead of him.
>
> The next car that came by was driven by an outspoken local atheist who had never been to church in his life. When he saw the family's distress, he took them into his own car. After inquiring as to their need, he took them to a local motel where he paid for a week's lodging while the father found work. He also paid for the father to rent a car so that he could look for work and gave the mother cash for food and new clothes.[1]

Get the point? Framed in these contemporary terms, the story is not only memorable; it's provocative in the same way that it provoked the first-century Jewish audience. Indeed, it's offensive, but its offensiveness finally gets us to think. In fact, I'd bet if this contemporary version of the parable were told this coming Sunday at churches across America, two things would happen: (1) some people would not return to their churches the following Sunday, and (2) those who did return would be thinking differently about themselves and others. I suspect that they'd be open to hearing more about this "new" teaching (in fact, many would be demanding it!), and our pastors would have a unique opportunity to preach a life-changing message to their most attentive audience ever. Pastors would be in a remarkable and rare position to have significant influence over normally complacent congregants.

That's the power of a great story. It provokes as it proffers. It prods as it progresses. It shakes people from their comfort zones and gets them asking questions they've never considered asking.

A great story shakes people from their comfort zones and gets them asking questions they've never considered asking.

Have you heard stories like that? Or told them? You probably have on occasion, so you know what I'm talking about.

But are you willing to try to use this approach more often now? It's surely worth the effort. As we said above, of all the principles covered in this study, other than prayer, storytelling may be the one most likely to stimulate change. Since people are so prone to *really* listening when we're telling a story, storytelling influences in the most nonthreatening and disarming of ways. Before we know it, we're face-to-face with an uncomfortable truth—one that will shadow us even when we try to run from it!

Make a habit of telling more stories in your efforts to persuade. Invest the time to identify stories that could be wake-up calls for those you're trying to influence. And invest the time to become a better storyteller by developing a delivery that's both enjoyable and enlightening. It's a technique that works in nurseries and nursing homes alike and everywhere in between. So, like Jesus, if you want to master the art of persuasion, master the art of storytelling.

Mastering the Art of Storytelling

We can look to many other places in Scripture where a story led to influence and change. To cite just a couple, think about how Nathan influenced King David to see the egregiousness of his sin: through a story (2 Sam. 12). Think of how Paul evangelized the Gentile world: through telling and retelling the story of his Damascus Road experience (e.g., Acts 22:6–21; 26:12–18). Overall, think of how God chose to reveal who he is and how he desires for us to live: through stories in the Bible.

Pretty compelling evidence that we should perfect our storytelling, don't you think? To improve the skills you already have, consider these practical tips:

Selecting a Story and Preparing to Tell It

- Finding an appropriate story is sometimes the hardest part. To do this, it helps to identify a situation in the past that's analogous to what you want to teach. In other words, identify a story where the change you'd like to see has already happened somewhere. Learn as much as you can about that situation and then tell that story. The more analogous the story

to your current situation, the more believable your
point will be and the more likely the story will be
influential.

- It's usually best for a story to have only one protagonist rather than a lot of them. Listeners can
connect well with a single character, empathize
with him or her, and thereby learn the lesson of the
story better.

- Practice telling the story. Then, if you really want
this to be effective, practice it some more. That
might sound weird, especially if you tell a lot of
stories. But truly great storytelling doesn't just
happen, not even for professionals. As with any
performance, excellence requires that you rehearse
before going "on stage" with your story.

Telling the Story

- As you're telling the story, relive it as well as you
can. If you imagine yourself in the setting you're
describing, you'll be more comfortable telling the
story, you'll include richer detail, and you'll tell it
in a way that draws others into that setting with
you. By contrast, when we tell a story by mentally
remembering how we've told it before, and then try
to repeat that earlier performance, our story usually falls flat.

- Perform the story. Tell it with emotion. Tell it with
enthusiasm and animation, using hand gestures
and other nonverbal cues. Use inflection in your
voice rather than a monotone delivery, and vary
your pace of delivery, slowing down in the most
important parts. If you can mentally "relive" the
story as you're telling it, as noted above, these
things will happen more naturally.

- Enjoy telling the story. Have fun with it. Don't worry about what anyone thinks of you.
- Avoid offering unnecessary details or tangents in the story. Practice helps you to identify these.
- Tell the story often. The best influencers tell good stories over and over again, even to people who have heard them before (like their employees or their kids). Why? Because people forget the lessons. A year after telling my son the Genghis Khan story, for example, he had remembered it differently—Khan was out hunting with his pet dog (not his hawk), they caught a snake, and everyone lived happily ever after. Ouch. Because I neglected to retell the story enough times, the anger management lesson was completely lost.
- Remember that storytelling is contagious. When people hear stories, they often want to continue the conversation by telling their own similar stories. This helps *immensely* in an influence situation. If the person you're trying to persuade connects enough with your story to tell you one with a similar lesson, then stop talking and listen attentively. People are convinced best when they convince themselves.

Some Other Tips

- Self-depreciating stories—stories about how you personally failed at something—tend to keep people's attention and they lend credibility to what you're saying.
- For any situation you encounter often (such as introducing yourself, telling someone about God, or training a new employee), have a stock story or two that you've polished and perfected. Few people can tell inspiring, motivating, or life-changing stories in an impromptu, off-the-cuff manner.

- There's not one right way to do this or even two or three. Find a storytelling style with which you're comfortable and stick with that. If something in the above list doesn't work for you, ignore it and do something else. What's important is that your storytelling style is entirely yours and that you're comfortable delivering in story form the messages that God wants you to deliver.

For Reflection

The "tell a story" principle says that stories persuade because they captivate, inspire, and stay with us. Take a few moments to reflect in your journal some thoughts related to these questions: Where have you seen this principle in operation? Do you know someone who is particularly good at telling stories? What characteristics do these people exhibit as they tell their stories? What characteristics do their stories have?

Think about the greatest influence challenge or challenges in your life and then respond to the following question: What stories can I tell that will get my point across in a memorable and emotional way? Take a few moments to reflect on a story that you can use. Then write it in your journal. Skip some lines so that you can go back and add details later.

— PRINCIPLE 8 —

Construct a Contrast

Picture this: a fanatical and militant group of men are determined to stone a woman to death, publicly and brutally. They chase her through the streets as she screams for her life. Onlookers do nothing except for the few who eagerly join the swarm of sadists.

Finally, with her bloody bare feet unable to take another step, the woman stumbles and falls, mere yards from where you sit. The executioners surround her, hurling insults before they hurl their rocks. "You're an adulteress!" they shriek. "A dirty whore! The law of Moses demands that you be killed!"

Oddly enough, before they carry out their sentence, the leader of the lynch mob turns to you for your advice. Well, sort of. Actually, he's not really interested in your advice; he's just hoping that you'll say something that contravenes their tradition so they can put you on death row, too.

"This woman's been caught in the act of adultery," he explains to you, "and under our law she's to be stoned to death. What do *you* say?"

Well, what *do* you say? A dozen angry men, well-armed and ready to fire, and their leader asks for your opinion, only so he can reject it. Meanwhile, the accused lies weeping at your feet. If ever there were a time to have influence skills, this would be it.

Now take this one step further. Imagine that you're such an effective influencer that merely one sentence out of your mouth saves the woman's life, disperses the crowd, and sends you safely on your way. How valuable would it be to have that sort of ability? How much good could you do with talent like that? How much could that gift, in the right hands (or mouth, for that matter), advance the kingdom of God?

> When you understand why Jesus' one line was so influential, you'll have at your disposal one of the most potent of persuasion practices: contrast.

It may be the most stunning example of influence in the entire Bible. You probably remember that moment of truth when Jesus was asked, "What should we do?" And you probably remember the single line of truth that Jesus spoke as he sat in the sand beneath them—a line that caused them to drop their weapons: *"The one without sin among you should be the first to throw a stone at her"* (John 8:7).

The would-be assassins looked down at him in disbelief. Then, reluctantly, they complied: "When they heard this, they left one by one, starting with the older men. Only He was left, with the woman" (John 8:9).

Like I said, it's arguably the most profound and dramatic example of influence in all of Scripture. Do you understand, though, *why* Jesus' one line was so influential? Once you do, you'll have at your disposal one of the most potent of persuasion practices: contrast.

The Power of Contrast

The contrast principle is easy to understand, and it's also one of the easiest influence principles to use. In a sentence, it's this: *The difference between things greatly influences our perceptions and decisions.* How we feel about a situation, an idea, a person, or a product depends on our benchmark, our reference point—the thing to which we're comparing it.

That may seem a little abstract, so let me give you a few everyday examples. When we look at the price tags on clothing or other goods, they say something like: "Their price: $50, Our price: $39.99." Contrasted against a reference point of fifty bucks, $39.99 may seem like a good deal to us.

When you walk into a furniture store, you'll encounter the more expensive items first and then the less expensive items farther back in the store. Why? Contrast. After seeing a $2,500 living room set, $999 doesn't seem so bad. Had the store arranged its products from low price to high price, the contrast principle would reduce rather than enhance sales.

Another example: When buying a diamond, you'll rarely see one on a white background. On what does every diamond sit in almost every jewelry store? A black background, right? The visual contrast makes it look far more dazzling.

The difference between things greatly influences our perceptions and decisions.

This is not just a principle for salespeople, though. We see the contrast principle in operation, sadly, through the growing problem of Internet pornography. Against the backdrop of younger, thinner, less inhibited women, a guy's view of his wife changes—guaranteed. "She just doesn't measure up," he thinks. "Not even close. She's not nearly as attractive or exciting as so many other women out there in the world. *I really got ripped off.*"

He might as well feed poison to the marriage. The cyber-contrast has the same toxic effect.

However, the principle can work just as powerfully to strengthen our relationships. When we almost lose someone we care about—or even if we genuinely think about that possibility—we get a chilling glimpse of what life would be like without that person. How much *worse* things could be becomes our new reference point, eclipsing the old reference point of how much *better* things could be. As a result, appreciation floods the relationship and it may be a long time before we again take this person for granted.

Contrast can change more than relationships, too; it can change minds. I had a professor in seminary who used this approach often when lecturing. For many controversial topics, he'd describe in nonpejorative, value-neutral terms, the far right and far left positions. Then he'd come to *his* position on the issue, a position that almost always sat comfortably between the two extremes. It was a compelling rhetorical approach. Contrasted against the extremes, his more moderate perspective seemed reasonable—and thereby persuasive.

Jesus' Use of Contrast

On that foundation let's come back full circle to the men preparing to exact vigilante justice on the woman at Jesus' feet. His one sentence cleared the crowd, without threat, without bribe, without emotion. Jesus influenced them simply through contrast, nothing more. One moment they were comparing her behavior to the Law of Moses; the next moment they were comparing her behavior to their own. Jesus changed their frame of reference, and in doing so he changed how they saw the situation.

Jesus used this same approach in other influence situations as well. Do you recall the story of the paralytic brought before Jesus and the scribes in Matthew 9? Jesus looks at the man with love and compassion, and then, to the utter horror of the nearby scribes, says to him: "Have courage, son, your sins are forgiven" (9:2).

> Jesus changed their frame of reference, and in doing so he changed how they saw the situation.

Look at what happened next, keeping in mind the contrast principle:

> At this, some of the scribes said among themselves, "He's blaspheming!"
> But perceiving their thoughts, Jesus said, "Why are you thinking evil things in your hearts? For which is easier: to say, 'Your sins are forgiven,' or to say, 'Get up and walk'? But so you may know that the Son of Man has authority on earth to forgive sins"—then He told the paralytic, "Get up, pick up your stretcher, and go home." And he got up and went home. When the crowds saw this, they were awestruck and gave glory to God who had given such authority to men. (9:3–8)

Notice a few things here. Jesus wants to influence their understanding of his ministry ("so you may know that the Son of Man has the authority on earth to forgive sins"). He pursues this influence through contrast. If he can do something greater such as healing a paralyzed man, he can do something lesser, such as forgiving the man's sins. And, at least for "the crowds," it works.

With a different crowd, a crowd on the Mount, Jesus again used contrast to influence them—and us—not to worry about so many things:

This is why I tell you: Don't worry about your life, what you will eat or what you will drink; or about your body, what you will wear. Isn't life more than food and the body more than clothing? Look at the birds of the sky: they don't sow or reap or gather into barns, yet your heavenly Father feeds them. Aren't you worth more than they? Can any of you add a single cubit to his height by worrying? And why do you worry about clothes? Learn how the wildflowers of the field grow: they don't labor or spin thread. Yet I tell you that not even Solomon in all his splendor was adorned like one of these! If that's how God clothes the grass of the field, which is here today and thrown into the furnace tomorrow, won't He do much more for you—you of little faith? (Matt. 6:25–30)

See the contrast principle at work in his words? Here's a one-second quiz: Where is it?

It's in two places. First, if God feeds the birds, how much more will he feed you? And second, if God clothes the flowers and fields, how much more will he clothe you? Just like he did with the vigilantes and with the scribes, Jesus reframes the anxiety of those on the mountainside in a new context—a context that has the potential to forever change the way they think.

Paul's Use of Contrast

Speaking of thought-changing, life-improving contrasts, let's not leave this topic without at least a brief look at how Paul used this influence principle.

Romans 8:18 is a life verse for many and for good reason. If we'd just align our thinking with this single verse, everything—*everything*—would be better in our lives. That probably sounds like an oversell (something that I really dislike, by the way, especially when listening to someone's exegesis), but I don't think it is in this instance. Think about the verse: "For I consider that the sufferings of this present time are not worth comparing with the glory that is going to be revealed to us."

By now you'll no doubt recognize the inherent, influential contrast in the verse. The first part of the verse is set against the second part; that is, the temporal sufferings we experience are set against an eternal life in paradise.

That mattered a whole lot to the original audience, a group of severely persecuted Roman Christians. Paul didn't tell this group to combat persecution or to run from it. He taught them to think about it differently, to keep it in proper perspective, to contrast it with an infinite inheritance of joy.

Paul taught us to think about persecution differently, to keep it in proper perspective, to contrast it with an infinite inheritance of joy.

Think of the remarkably practical applications of this teaching. If a friend is struggling with the ordinary stuff of daily life—for instance, a misbehaving toddler, an awful commute, an impossible coworker, a relentless schedule— some humble Romans 8:18 counsel might encourage your friend to take a longer view of things, to see the present day in eternal context and to set her burdens against the bigger picture of how blessed she really is. "That's annoying, for sure," you might say, "but maybe you can try to see it as little stuff compared to what really matters. Sure it's important to deal with it, and I'll help you think through that, but try to keep it in proper perspective. We're blessed so abundantly."

This is the contrast principle at its best. But one word of advice, if I could: before you try to encourage a friend with it, let God use it in you first. Keep regular reminders in front of you that will contrast the day's burdens against God's past, current, and future blessings. Maintain this frame of mind to reap more gratitude and joy, fewer conflicts, the surprising ability to forgive, and the peace that's been so elusive in your life. And if that isn't enough, in doing so, you'll also lay the foundation to influence your friend more authentically, *out of personal experience with this God-given approach.*

This contrast principle is not some mind trick. It's nothing less than a biblically-based pathway to a better life and to influencing others to walk this pathway with you, with Paul, and with Jesus.

Perhaps your friend will think that's some pretty good company!

For Reflection

The "construct a contrast" principle says that the difference between things greatly influences our perceptions and decisions. Where have you seen this principle in operation? Can you think of any particular contrasts that have changed your way of thinking? Take a few moments to write them down in your journal.

Think about the greatest influence challenge or challenges in your life. Is there something to which this option compares favorably? Can you use a contrast to show how much worse things could be in that person's life? Jot down some possible contrasts between the present situation and what the situation might be and save them for possible use in your future conversations.

— PRINCIPLE 9 —

Find a Metaphor

I'm at a crossroads.

My car is a lemon.

She's sharp as a tack.

Twenty-three hundred years ago Aristotle, who's considered the father of persuasion theory, wrote in his book, *Poetics*: "The greatest thing by far is to be a master of metaphor." Similarly, in *Rhetoric*, he taught that "from metaphor we can best get hold of something fresh."

Kids really blossom at that school.

He's an old flame.

I've got too much on my plate right now.

The ancient philosopher defined *metaphor* quite aptly as "the act of giving a thing a name that belongs to something else." As such, a metaphor can help us to see things in a new way, perhaps in a way we hadn't seen them before. That's why it's such a powerful influencer. Clever and timely use of metaphors can fundamentally alter the way people think about something.

Business is war.

My home is a zoo.

I'm drowning in work.

You're the light of my life.

The tyrants of political correctness on campus.

Each one of these sentences or phrases paints a picture, doesn't it? Some of the pictures may even be vivid and memorable enough to reorient our perspective. Take the "business is war" metaphor, for example. It's a reasonably common way of thinking and talking about the business world, but it also turns out to be a *dangerously* common way. There's actually some solid research that shows that businesspeople who think in these "war" terms are more likely to do unethical things, like steal from a competitor, than are those who operate under a different metaphor, like "business is a race."

That's a profound finding. It seems that we could improve business ethics without ever spending a dime. Just change the metaphor by which people operate.

But well beyond that business context, the same kind of reorientation can apply to just about every other area of our life. If, say, a man thinks of himself not as a "father" (which may be fraught with all sorts of baggage from his own upbringing) but primarily as a "teacher," his level of patience and his disposition toward his kids may change instantly. Why not give it a try tonight, guys? And if a Christian employee thinks of her job not as "work," but as her "ministry," how she uses her time and how hard she works will likely change for the better. Similarly, if she thinks of herself not as an "employee" but as an "ambassador for God," her workplace attitude and character might change, as well.

A well-chosen metaphor can, in a covert and nonthreatening way, completely reorient a person's perspective.

The point is this: our frame of reference matters. As we saw in the previous chapter, a person's context often determines how he or she behaves. A well-chosen metaphor can, in a covert and nonthreatening way, shift that context, opening the door to lasting change. But don't take my word for it. Or Aristotle's, for that matter. Take your cue from someone even smarter than Aristotle.

Jesus' Metaphors

Think about the various metaphors Jesus used and how colorful and even provocative they are. In fact, before you read on, look away from the page for a minute and see if you can recall some of them. There are a bunch.

Here's the first one that often rolls off of people's lips when I ask this question: Jesus called the religious leaders of the day "whitewashed tombs." Remember that? It's in Matthew 23:27. What a scandalous thing to say! And what tremendous potential it had to adjust the way people thought about their leadership. These aren't authoritative sages to be followed and revered. They're *whitewashed tombs*—sparkling clean and perfect on the outside, dead and rotting on the inside. Could anyone hearing these words ever look at a Pharisee the same way again? More likely, people would forever associate the leaders' pristine robes with superficiality, veneer, and hypocrisy. All that from two words!

That's what a wise metaphor does: it can change the way we see something, no matter how many times we've seen it or thought about it before.

> Could anyone hearing Jesus' metaphor—"whitewashed tombs"—ever look at a Pharisee the same way again?

Maybe that's why Jesus gives us so many metaphors about himself, to give the people of his day (and us) fresh perspective about how to experience God. Jesus calls himself the "good shepherd"—a kind guide. He's "the gate" and "the door"—something through which we need to go. He's "the bread of life"—something one would take in for nourishment. He's "the vine"—something to which we "branches" must remain connected. He's "the way, the truth, and the life"—a person we need to follow if we want our life sustained.

Each of these metaphors shapes our perception of Jesus in a way that straightforward assertions simply cannot. The same with Jesus' metaphors for some of the central issues of his ministry: "faith" and "the kingdom of God." Regarding faith, Jesus taught that all we need is a little to do a lot—the faith of a "mustard seed," the smallest seed that grows into the biggest tree. And he communicated the value of the kingdom of God by likening it to "a treasure in a field" or "a pearl of great price." Any more questions about its value?

Paul's Metaphors

Paul piggybacked on this approach. Among his most cited behavior-changing metaphors is the race image of the Christian life. Remember that? To exhort the Corinthians to make their faith life a continuing priority, he connects it metaphorically to something commonplace in Greek culture: "Do you not know that the runners in a stadium all race, but only one receives the prize? Run in such a way that you may win" (1 Cor. 9:24). He returns to the image elsewhere in his writings, including his swan song to Timothy: "I have fought the good fight, I have finished the race, I have kept the faith" (2 Tim. 4:7).

Does this kind of metaphor matter? You bet! If we think of our faith journey as a race, we're more likely to keep pressing forward, instead of snoozing for a season like Aesop's fabled hare.

Paul uses metaphor to keep us in right relation with one another as well. Think about his "body" metaphor in his first letter to the Corinthians. To this people rife with arrogance and pride, individuals prone to thinking themselves better than those around them, Paul offers an essential and timeless corrective based on a common context that everyone has. He reminds them that though the body is made up of many parts, it's still one body with parts arranged and connected just the way God designed them to be:

> "The eye cannot say to the hand, 'I don't need you!' nor again the head to the feet, 'I don't need you!' On the contrary, all the more, those parts of the body that seem to be weaker are necessary."
> (1 Cor. 12:21–22)

Notice that he doesn't just come out and say, "Shut up about how great you are!" He takes a softer, subtler approach—an important tactic with prideful people—that leverages the power of metaphor to change the way they think about one another.

Paul doesn't say to the Corinthians: "Shut up about how great you are!" He uses the softer, subtler approach of metaphor—an important tactic with prideful people.

If you're a regular reader of the New Testament, you can probably think of other Pauline masterpieces. When cautioning the Corinthians not to tolerate sin in their congregation, he wrote: "Don't you know that a little yeast permeates the whole batch of dough?" (1 Cor. 5:6). When encouraging the Ephesians to take a stand against Satan's schemes, he told them to "put on the full armor of God," including things like the belt of truth, the "shield of faith," the "helmet of salvation," and the "sword of the Spirit" (Eph. 6:11–17 NIV). These are not attempts at poetry;

they're attempts to change behavior through the creative use of metaphor. And two millennia later, they're still doing just that.

Make the Effort to Find a Metaphor

Someone once said, "Metaphors show us that the world is full of cousins." Come to think of it, that is sort of a metaphor about metaphors! Anyway, the point of this chapter is that we should look for those cousins, those connections between things that can make the difference between influencing somebody or not, between a change in their behavior or more of the same, between getting them on God's agenda or remaining on their own.

Is it worth the mental effort to find a metaphor? Jesus thought so. Paul thought so. James thought so (the tongue is a rudder, James 3:4–5). Solomon thought so (guard your heart, for it is the wellspring of life, Proverbs 4:23 NIV). John thought so (God is love, 1 John 4:8).

Shouldn't we think so, too?

For Reflection

The "find a metaphor" principle says that metaphor, showing that one thing resembles another thing, can cause people to see and think in new ways. People use metaphor in everyday conversation, sometimes in relation to the most mundane aspects of life. Where have you seen this principle in operation?

Think about the greatest influence challenge or challenges in your life. Is there a metaphor you can use that will encourage this person to see the situation differently? Jot down a few possibilities that you may be able to use when you next talk to that person.

PART 4

Offer Compelling Evidence

You may have heard the term *postmodern* being thrown around these days. Perhaps you've even heard it or used it in the circles in which you travel. It's a critically important concept for us to understand if we're serious about becoming better influencers.

Postmodern is a term that tries to capture how people think these days—their assumptions about what's true and untrue, what's right and wrong, what's believable and unbelievable. For centuries the Christian worldview had the market cornered on these things, at least in the Western world. What was true and right and believable depended on what the church said or, later for some, what the Bible said.

During a period in the eighteenth century that we now call "The Enlightenment," these Christian assumptions were challenged incessantly by people who claimed that what's true is what's *provable* and *rational*—words they said didn't apply to an alleged supernatural realm of God and angels and incarnate beings. As a result, a competing brand emerged for people's hearts and minds in the eighteenth century, a brand we now call *modernism*, which caused many to think differently about right and wrong and about the credibility of the Christian faith.

Persuasion required proof—empirical proof or some other rational basis for belief. As a result, through the nineteenth and twentieth centuries, the sciences and the universities became the means for our redemption, supplanting "unprovable" and "irrational" assumptions about God, a sacrificed Son, a Holy Spirit, and an inspired Bible. Such concepts were increasingly dismissed as superstition or at best unknowable.

Stay with me here. Although this is merely a basic sociological sketch, it's essential information for any influence-minded Christian. Return now to this term *postmodern*. It implies that we've moved beyond the assumptions of modernism (just like the term *modernism* implied that we moved beyond what came before it). In some ways postmodernism is a good thing; no longer do we slavishly assume that what's right or true is limited to what's provable through observation. That reopens the door to belief in an invisible Creator and his call on our life. But the downside of postmodern thought is that as a culture we've slid from the dogmatic "truth is what's provable" to the dogmatic "truth is relative."

Ever hear that claim? You probably have since it's commonplace, especially when Christians make a claim to absolute truth—the claim that there are absolutes that should guide every aspect of our lives. What seemed obvious just a few centuries ago is now considered radical and arrogant, even dangerous.

If you've ever sought to convince anyone in the Western world of the truth of Christianity or the reliability of the Gospels, you've no doubt run into this sort of relativistic thinking. It's subtle but it's rampant. It drives what people believe and what they do, and, importantly for our context, it drives what they consider persuasive.

For people in a postmodern mind-set—and they're not just pipe-smoking, tweed-jacketed, ivory-tower professors but the ordinary people with whom you rub shoulders every day—skepticism has become a way of life. Saddled with the assumption that there's no such thing as absolute truth (what's true for you may not be true for me), who wouldn't be skeptical of any truth claim these days? It's even infected countless people who sit in the pews around you every weekend.

You know people like this, right? Probably a lot of people like this—people who are chronic doubters, who are always asking for proof, who may need to experience something for themselves before they can make a judgment about its validity or who roll their eyes when you mention the Bible. This is the fruit of postmodernism, and there's a cornucopia of it around you daily.

What does this mean for Christians who seek to be effective persuaders? A whole lot. Armed with this knowledge about our audience (recall Principle 3), we understand the necessity to have more than stories or service or similarity to persuade some people. The principles already covered in this book, powerful as they are, may not be enough to move some people along to a new way of thinking. Many people today insist on solid, compelling evidence before they embrace new ideas or new behaviors.

This section will discuss three types of evidence that persuades people who are marinated in today's culture. These are not the only kinds of evidence that exist, mind you, but they're three that Jesus used with great success. You see, even two thousand years ago, long before people became enlightened, modern, or postmodern, these three kinds of evidence changed hearts and minds. How much more so are they required today?

In familiar Gospel stories we see Jesus using *authoritative evidence*, *experiential evidence*, and *social evidence* to influence those around him. So let's look now at what each of these entails, how Jesus used them, and how we can follow his lead to become more influential, even with the most resistant of audiences.

— PRINCIPLE 10 —

Use Authoritative Evidence

They were heavy-handed and arrogant, scoffing at the rabble that surrounded them in the temple. They had their lackeys push people out of the way so they could walk down the street unimpeded. They adorned themselves with special clothing and further set themselves apart with reserved seats, pristine robes, and lengthy tassels. They even wore devices called *phylacteries* on their foreheads—boxes with long Scripture verses on them, some of them so long that the wearer looked like a unicorn!

The elaborate getups might have seemed like Halloween costumes to our modern eyes, but to the people who observed them, they were flamboyant displays that declared, "I'm better than you." No treats here; only tricks. These men were their spiritual leaders, interpreters of the law and the apparent gateway to heaven; and they led their followers into a burdensome, oppressive lifestyle that alienated people from both God and one another.

If Jesus is to be believed, some of the religious leaders of his day were truly scoundrels. Listen to his startling indictment of them in Matthew 23:

> "[You] tie up heavy loads that are hard to
> carry and put them on people's shoulders, but
> [you yourselves] aren't willing to lift a finger to
> move them. [You] do everything to be observed
> by others. . . . You lock up the kingdom of heaven
> from people. . . . You don't go in, and you don't

allow those entering to go in. . . . You devour wid-
ows' houses and make long prayers just for
show. . . . [You] are full of greed and self-
indulgence! . . . You are full of hypocrisy and
lawlessness." (vv. 4–5, 13–14, 25, 28)

Ironically and tragically, the chief priests were the chief
impediments to people's relationship with God. Is it any
wonder that Jesus ultimately condemns this group (note
the use of metaphors) as "snakes" and a "brood of vipers"
(v. 33)?

Hardly. What is a wonder, though, is that so many
people willingly followed these guys. Why follow pompous
hypocrites who repaid allegiance with affliction? Why be
influenced by such people?

In a word, *authority*. People considered the religious
leaders of the day to be authorities on interpretation and all
things spiritual. As such, they willingly followed these pied
pipers of Palestine into a life of hardship and misery.

We can state the lesson in Principle 10 this way: Rightly
or wrongly, people usually follow authority—experts and
those who offer expert advice. And, like all of these influence principles, this one can work just as powerfully for
good as it does for evil. We'll see that in a minute. But let's
unpack the concept a little more first.

We Are Influenced by Authoritative Evidence

From early in our childhood, we're conditioned to
obey, or at least respect, authority: parents, teachers,
coaches, police officers, pastors, you name it. Legitimate
authorities abound when you're six years old. But they also
abound when you're twenty-six, fifty-six, and ninety-six.
Moreover, signals of authority, such as credentials, position, title, knowledge—even the quality of their houses,

clothing, or cars—become shortcuts for us to decide whether we should defer to them.

Have you noticed this? Many people deny that they do it, but experiment after experiment shows almost *everyone* does this, usually subconsciously. When we want to know the best course of action, we often look to the opinions of experts. Want to know how to get your kid to behave? Get a parenting book. Hoping for a better marriage? Visit an expert's Web site on marital bliss. Want to know how to make that initiative at work successful? Benchmark someone who's already done it successfully. Want to know which car to purchase? Read the ratings from the objective third parties who hand out the awards. Looking for the path to spiritual fulfillment? Chat with a pastor.

> When we want to know the best course of action, we often look to the opinions of experts.

In fact, I suspect that you'd be amazed if you went through this day—just this one day—taking inventory of the number of times seemingly authoritative advice influences people's thinking. (My hope is that you might even include this chapter in that list!) To get you started, look at the list I compiled over the past couple hours:

- On that back of a book I'm reading, I found endorsements—glowing statements about the book from people with impressive titles. It's a boring book, but with authority figures like these singing the praises of a book, I feel the tug to read it a little more closely.
- While surfing the Web, I stumbled across information intended to discourage teenagers from smoking. It cites authorities like the U.S. Surgeon

General and the American Cancer Society to make its case.

- I hear the TV in the next room blaring something about how the critics are raving about how "progressive" and "creative" some new movie is. The ad's trying to leverage the critics' seeming expertise, of course.

- I was about to say to one of my kids: "Tell your brother to turn down the TV." Instead, I chose to frame the request a bit differently: "Tell your brother that Dad wants him to turn down the TV." The TV got turned down rather quickly.

- I turn back to the computer to find that a professor in another department has sent me an e-mail: "The VP asked me to pull a team together to evaluate the undergraduate curriculum. Can I count on your help?" I say yes even though I don't have the time. It's the vice president, after all.

- Later I glance at the newspaper. One article notes that "a major study has connected workplace stress to heart disease and shorter life spans." The study is from a leading research university, adding to the credibility of the findings. I vow to reevaluate my level of workplace stress (right after I'm done with the curriculum committee assignment).

Jesus' Use of the Authority Principle

As you see, this is a timeless influence principle, as powerful in the twenty-first century as it was in the first. Let's return to that earlier time for a moment. Did you ever notice that Jesus used this authority principle quite a bit? Think about his ministry, about the things that *really* seemed to convince people that Jesus was different, something special, someone worth listening to. What convinced them the most?

That's a hard question, since there were a lot of things, but for many people what comes to mind is Jesus' miracles—turning water to wine, feeding thousands from a few loaves and fish, healing the paralyzed and blind, calming storms, raising the dead. Who, after witnessing such an event, could resist following him? Who, after hearing about such an event, could resist seeing for themselves what Jesus was all about?

Jesus' miracles are classic examples of authoritative evidence at work.

Jesus' miracles are classic examples of authoritative evidence at work. People who perform bona fide miracles must be authorities, right? As a result, we're naturally drawn to them, we're more likely to listen to them, and in this case we're more likely to embrace this person's radical claims to be God.

What about Jesus' use of the authority principle beyond the miracles? Consider for a moment the way he taught. His words and tone were more compelling than others' because "He was teaching them like one who had authority, and not like their scribes" (Matt. 7:29). Mark says it through the mouths of the people themselves: "They were all amazed, so they began to argue with one another, saying, 'What is this? A new teaching with authority!'" (Mark 1:27–28). Authoritative communication breeds influence.

We can go even further than this. Remember when Jesus was in the desert preparing for his ministry? He was tempted by Satan repeatedly with offers that some of us, especially in a severely weakened state, would find irresistible—promises of power and riches, not to mention food (not a trivial temptation after forty days without a meal). How did Jesus respond? Not by running from temptation like Joseph from Potipher's wife. And not just with a rebuke like: "No Satan, go to hell." But instead, Jesus responded with authoritative evidence, namely Scripture.

When Satan said: "Tell these stones to become bread," Jesus replied with a passage from Deuteronomy: "'Man must not live on bread alone but on every word that comes from the mouth of God'" (Matt. 4:3–4, quoting Deut. 8:3). When Satan said, "If You are the Son of God, prove it by surviving a jump from the top of this mountain," Jesus returned to Deuteronomy: "'Do not test the Lord your God'" (Matt. 4:7, quoting Deut. 6:16). And when Satan made his last-ditch effort by promising all the kingdoms of the world if Jesus would worship him, Jesus admonished him with Scripture once again: "Go away Satan! For it is written: 'Worship the Lord your God, and serve him only'" (Matt. 4:10, quoting Deut. 6:13).

> How did Jesus respond to Satan in the desert? With authoritative evidence, namely Scripture.

This is significant. Jesus could have responded in countless ways to the bait, but he chose to rely on the authority of Scripture. Let me suggest something: I think Jesus' words were meant to influence those of us who would hear the story throughout the centuries much more than they were meant to influence Satan. What more authoritative evidence could one possibly give in tough situations than the Word of God? We need to be discerning how we use Scripture to persuade, of course, but with some audiences it's going to be the turning point so we should rely on it. The authoritative evidence of the Bible is an essential pathway to persuasion.

Interested in some additional examples of this principle in action in Scripture? There are many more, for better or worse:

- Without protest or even comment, Abraham was willing to kill his beloved son Isaac because God asked him to do so. God's authority was enough to secure Abraham's compliance.

- The people of Israel convinced themselves to select a man named Saul to be their king because he had some of the trappings of authority—height, strength, and good looks. Good principle but a bad application.

- Throughout his Gospel, Matthew cites the authority of Old Testament prophesy to convince the Jews that Jesus is the promised Messiah.

- Jesus instructs his followers to commandeer a donkey and a colt, instructing them that "if anyone says anything to you, you should say that the Lord needs them" (Matt. 21:3). It doesn't get more authoritative than that, does it?

Practical Tips for Using Authoritative Evidence

Are you ready to try this one out? It's not hard to do. In fact, you probably do it several times a day already without even thinking about it. We know people are convinced by authoritative evidence so we offer it a lot.

To supplement what you already know, here are some quick words of counsel as you road test this principle:

- Authoritative evidence is almost always available for our attempts at influence. Look for it in several

places: subject matter experts, laws, research findings, the comments of respected people, "the boss,"
company policy, best-selling books, and, where
appropriate, the Judeo-Christian Scriptures.

- Be sure the authoritative evidence you're using *is
considered authoritative by the person you're trying to
influence*. Often we make the mistake of quoting
sources and authorities that are meaningful to us
but irrelevant to the person to whom we're speaking. A typical example of this is using "The Bible
says . . ." to someone who does not believe the
Bible is the authoritative Word of God.

- People are constantly thinking, *why should I believe
you?* So give them a reason. Don't hesitate to communicate, at least subtly, your own authority or
credentials on an issue, if you have some. Your
education, skills, experience, and other gifts may
go a long way toward keeping someone listening
and toward encouraging him or her to consider
your point of view.

- When appropriate, dress in an authoritative manner and even use a higher-level vocabulary. You'll
be amazed at how a few twenty-dollar words can
lead to more deference.

For Reflection

The "authoritative evidence" principle says that we're
influenced by experts and credentials. Where have you
seen this principle in operation? Write down in your
notebook several examples of authorities to whom we
defer.

Think about the greatest influence challenge or challenges in your life and ask yourself the following questions:
Where have I demonstrated my expertise on this matter?

How can I point to other expert evidence that this person would find convincing? Are there other people whose opinion this person would respect?

— PRINCIPLE 11 —

Use Experiential Evidence

I hear the stories in my role as a management consultant, and I hear the stories from my MBA students. From time to time, I've even experienced the joy firsthand. It's remarkable how many naysayers, disrupters, and uncivil people there are in the workplace these days. And each one seems to have a Ph.D. in everything.

Know the profile? If you worked for pay for any length of time, you probably do. Get that person in mind for a minute—you know, the guy or gal who questioned and chastised everything you did, usually with a touch of attitude. The person who started every negotiation with no and worked from there. The person who, when told he or she was going to make a mistake, refused to listen to advice and then went on to make that very mistake.

Got the picture? Can you visualize this person, whether he or she was your boss, your employee, or a person at your level? Now think about this: How was this person ever persuaded about anything? Did reasoning work? Kindness? Storytelling or clever, frame-changing metaphors? If the person you're thinking of is like some of the gems in my mind, none of those approaches worked. *Nothing* ever seems to change their mind.

Of course, it's not just some of our coworkers who fit this profile of "unpersuadable." It might be a child, perhaps a teenager. It might be our spouse, someone at church, or the person living next door. The common thread is that this person is exceedingly difficult to persuade.

Some people are exceedingly difficult to persuade unless they experience something for themselves. And that's the key to influencing such people.

Except, that is, when they experience something for themselves. And that's the key to influencing such people.

Adopt Jesus' Approach to Persuading the Unpersuadable

Some people are simply never convinced unless they see for themselves the truth of the matter. They need to experience the benefit or the validity of an idea, especially one that does not fit neatly into their worldview or time commitments, before they can accept it. Some of them are so stubborn that they need to make a mistake before they'll consider whether they might be mistaken.

Experience seems to be their only teacher. So let it be. Adopt Jesus' approach to influencing that chronic doubter, that persistent pessimist, or that unpersuadable person at work or home or anywhere else.

Jesus' approach? You remember the story. You may have heard it dozens of times. The disciples are gathered in a room, still hiding out after Jesus' death, when Mary Magdalene comes running in with the astonishing news that Jesus is alive again. Soon thereafter Jesus himself appears to his friends and breathes the Holy Spirit into them. But one of the disciples, Thomas, wasn't there.

Here's how John recalls the moment:

So the other disciples kept telling him, "We
have seen the Lord!"

But he [Thomas] said to them, "If I don't see
the mark of the nails in His hands, put my finger
into the mark of the nails, and put my hand into
His side, I will never believe!" (John 20:25)

Unpersuadable. None of the influence principles we've
discussed in this study are working here. Telling Thomas
the story of Jesus' return wasn't enough (Principle 7).
The disciples' trustworthiness and similarity to Thomas
weren't enough (Principles 2 and 4). The social evidence
that several of them were saying the same thing to him
wasn't enough (Principle 12). Only one thing would persuade Thomas: experience. He had to see for himself.

Only one thing would persuade Thomas:
experience. He had to see for himself.
So Jesus showed him.

I suspect that Thomas might have been a difficult guy
to live with for the next eight days until Jesus returned
again. He might have even fit the profile of the person
you were thinking about a few minutes ago, insolent and
disbelieving. But then Jesus did reappear, this time with
Thomas in attendance. Can you see the expression on
Thomas's face?

In all likelihood, that sight alone was all that Thomas
needed to believe, but Jesus chose to give him the full
treatment:

Then He said to Thomas, "Put your finger here
and observe My hands. Reach out your hand and
put it into My side. Don't be an unbeliever, but a
believer."

> Thomas responded to Him, "My Lord and my
> God!" (John 20:27–28)

Poor guy. One little incident and he's forever labeled the doubter. Centuries later we still use the term "doubting Thomas" to describe a skeptical person. But before we're too hard on him, let's ask ourselves, *would we have really believed their story?* I'd like to think that I would have, but honestly, I'm not sure. I guess some things, especially things that call for a radical shift in our thinking, we just have to experience for ourselves.

Persuading Paul

That was the case some time later with a zealous Pharisee named Saul, who would later change his name to Paul. Talk about tough sell! It would be like convincing Bin Laden to become a Baptist. How in the world could Jesus persuade a man like this to go from incarcerating Christians to incubating them?

How did Jesus persuade a man like
Saul to go from incarcerating Christians
to incubating them? Experiential evidence.
He allowed Saul to see for himself
on the Damascus Road.

Only through personal experience. Jesus appeared personally to Saul as he was on his way to jail some more Christians:

> Meanwhile Saul, still breathing threats and
> murder against the disciples of the Lord, went
> to the high priest and requested letters from
> him to the synagogues in Damascus, so that if

he found any who belonged to the Way, either men or women, he might bring them as prisoners to Jerusalem. As he traveled and was nearing Damascus, a light from heaven suddenly flashed around him. Falling to the ground, he heard a voice saying to him, "Saul, Saul, why are you persecuting Me?"

"Who are You, Lord?" he said.

"I am Jesus, whom you are persecuting," He replied. "But get up and go into the city, and you will be told what you must do."

The men who were traveling with him stood speechless, hearing the sound but seeing no one. Then Saul got up from the ground, and though his eyes were open, he could see nothing. So they took him by the hand and led him into Damascus. He was unable to see for three days, and did not eat or drink. (Acts 9:1–9)

Soon after this Saul was baptized, took the Roman form of his name, Paul, and became the most prolific evangelist of his time, arguably of all time. I suspect that it never would have happened, though, if it hadn't been for his personal experience on the road to Damascus.

That's the power of experience, an influence method that we'd be wise to respect and perfect.

Experiential Evidence in the Old Testament

This can be a bit of an abstract principle, so to solidify our understanding, let's briefly consider a few other biblical examples. Each of these, from the Old Testament book of Daniel, illustrates experiential evidence in action.

In Daniel 1 we read the story of the Israelites being taken from Jerusalem to Babylonia. Among them was a boy named Daniel. But Daniel didn't live in hardship while in captivity. Based on his physical appearance and intelligence, he was one of the Israelites selected to be trained for the king's service. Also with him were three men whose names, though unusual, you might remember: Hananiah, Mishael, and Azariah (names that were later changed by the king to Shadrach, Meshach, and Abednego).

If you have to live as a slave, this is the way to do it: decent accommodations, luscious food and drink, and daily education in language and literature, and probably math, law, astronomy, architecture, and agriculture. Not exactly your father's captivity in Egypt. The only problem, though, was that the cuisine wasn't kosher. It had been sacrificed to pagan gods, and it contained foods that the one true God had prohibited his chosen people to eat.

The four boys did not want to be defiled by partaking of the food and, as a result, found themselves with an enormous influence challenge on their hands. With no power whatsoever and their very lives belonging to the king, how could they convince the guards to alter their diet?

Look at what they do, with an eye toward the "experiential evidence" principle:

> Daniel determined that he would not defile
> himself with the king's food or with the wine he
> drank. So he asked permission from the chief official not to defile himself. God had granted Daniel
> favor and compassion from the chief official, yet
> he said to Daniel, "My lord the king assigned your
> food and drink. I'm afraid of what would happen if
> he saw your faces looking thinner than those of the
> other young men your age. You would endanger
> my life with the king."
> So Daniel said to the guard whom the chief
> official had assigned to Daniel, Hananiah,
> Mishael, and Azariah, "Please test your servants
> for 10 days. Let us be given vegetables to eat and

water to drink. Then examine our appearance and
the appearance of the young men who are eating
the king's food, and deal with your servants based
on what you see." He agreed with them in this
matter and tested them for 10 days. At the end of
10 days they looked better and healthier than all
the young men who were eating the king's food. So
the guard continued to remove their food and the
wine they were to drink and gave them vegetables.
(Dan. 1:8–16)

Not a bad approach, eh? Daniel was intelligent, indeed.
He discerned that the only way the guard would grant his
unorthodox—even dangerous—request would be if the
guard saw for himself the wisdom of that request. The
guard had to experience the result, not just hear about it.
There needed to be some physical, tangible evidence for
the guard to be persuaded. So Daniel arranges for that
evidence with his ten-day trial. Nothing short of brilliant.

Daniel didn't comply with the king's
order and was offered up as feline
fricassee. But after experiencing Daniel's
deliverance, King Darius was completely
persuaded of God's supremacy.

The same experiential approach also served these men
well later on. In two of the most familiar stories in the Old
Testament, God-given experiential evidence becomes the
pathway to persuasion. When Shadrach, Meshach, and
Abednego refuse to bow down to King Nebuchadnezzar's
golden idol, their treason lands them in "a furnace of blaz-
ing fire" (Dan. 3:6). But their unshakable faith saves them
and they walk out unscathed, and the king, having experienced the power of God, says:

"Praise to the God of Shadrach, Meshach, and Abednego! He sent His angel and rescued His servants who trusted in Him. They violated the king's command and risked their lives rather than serve or worship any god except their own God. Therefore I issue a decree that anyone of any people, nation, or language who says anything offensive against the God of Shadrach, Meshach, and Abednego will be torn limb from limb and his house made a garbage dump. For there is no other god who is able to deliver like this." (Dan. 3:28–29)

Nothing would have convinced the king except seeing for himself, so God let him see.

Same with King Darius, who loved his servant Daniel but was cornered into throwing Daniel to the lions by his own decree: "Anyone who petitions any god or man except you, the king, will be thrown into the lions' den" (Dan. 6:7). Faithful Daniel could not comply, of course, and is flung down as feline fricassee. But after experiencing Daniel's deliverance—God's protection for an entire night with the lions—Darius was completely persuaded of God's supremacy. He even became something of an evangelist:

Then King Darius wrote to those of every people, nation, and language who live in all the earth: "May your prosperity abound. I issue a decree that in all my royal dominion, people must tremble in fear before the God of Daniel:

For He is the living God,
and He endures forever;
His kingdom will never be destroyed,
and His dominion has no end.
He rescues and delivers;
He performs signs and wonders

in the heavens and on the earth,
for He has rescued Daniel
from the power of the lions." (Dan. 6:25–27)

Influence through experience. With the smart, with the stubborn, with the powerful, with the skeptical—with the help of God—it's a pathway to persuasion.

And It's Not Just for the Tough Cases

The point of all this, of course, is that if you want to be a more effective influencer, learn how to use experiential evidence, particularly with those hard-to-convince folks. Also recognize, though, that these days this approach is helpful—sometimes even pivotal—in many other situations as well.

That's because we currently live in a "seeing is believing" culture. People are increasingly skeptical about the notion of truth, increasingly on guard against manipulators and sales gimmicks, and increasingly relying on personal experience as the consummate measure of right and wrong. As a result, it's becoming increasingly important to let people experience the benefit or truth of our ideas—not just hear about them—as part of our influence attempts.

Do more than just give reasons. Find a way to let people experience the benefit of change or the cost of the status quo.

Think back to your own experience just over this past week. Haven't you seen this principle in operation almost daily? It comes in the form of taste tests in grocery stores, free samples of fudge outside the candy shop, invitations by colleges to visit their campus on preview day, tempting dessert trays brought to your restaurant table near the end of your meal, fragrance ads in magazines that are more than a little aromatic, pro-life rallies that display graphic pictures of aborted babies, and free Internet samples of movie trailers, thirty-second music clips, productivity software, and video games.

The lesson for us is this: If you want people to change their minds, you may need to change your approach. Do more than just give reasons. Find a way to let these people experience the benefit of change or the cost of the status quo. It may not be immediately obvious how to do that, so invest some time to develop creative ideas. Put yourself in the other person's shoes and think about what might seem compelling. Solicit fresh ideas from smart friends. And most importantly, ask God to reveal a wise and effective approach. After all, he himself is an advocate of experiential evidence, encouraging us to "taste and see that the LORD is good" (Ps. 34:8).

For Reflection

The "experiential evidence" principle says that sometimes people will never be convinced unless they see it for themselves. Where have you seen this principle in operation? Have you been persuaded by it? Make some notes about places where you've observed it or been swayed by it, as well as names of the person or persons who used it.

Think about the greatest influence challenge or challenges in your life and then ask yourself a couple of questions: Can I get this person to experience the cost of the status quo or the benefit of changing it? What do I need to do for this to happen? Make some notes to prepare for the next time you talk to this person or persons.

— PRINCIPLE 12 —

Use Social Evidence

See if this doesn't sound familiar. You're in a department store trying to choose between two competing items. Sensing your dilemma, a smiling salesperson offers some help by indicating what the "most popular" item is. Curiously, that information pushes you off the fence; you buy what most other people have bought.

It happens in restaurants too, right? How many times have you heard a waiter or waitress tell you that some item is the most popular or best-selling item on the menu, or say something like "most people order the rice with that"?

Another example: You may do the same thing I do when buying books from an online bookseller. Did you ever look at the sales ranking for a book to get a clue about whether it's worthwhile? Ever read the comments by the amateur reviewers to help you make a decision? Rightly or wrongly, that seems to be my standard approach.

In each of these cases, "social evidence"—the behaviors of others—influences our decision. It's not automatically a good thing or a bad thing; it's just a shortcut we take in decision-making to help us sift through a world of choices. And as we'll see in a minute, we can learn a few things from the ministry of Jesus about its appropriate use.

First, though, let's get a more concrete grasp of the social evidence principle. We see it in operation all around us every day. A fast-food restaurant tells us on its sign how many billions the chain has served. A special interest group reports their latest poll numbers that support their cause, hoping to sway our opinion. A company boasts that it's the "fastest growing" firm in its industry to attract investors and customers alike. A Christian school displays a large placard of a thermometer, indicating how much money has been raised toward its fund-raising goal and encouraging you to give today.

Social evidence—the behavior of others—is a shortcut that we use in decision-making to help us sift through a world of choices.

The common thread among all these influence attempts? Each one seeks to affect our thinking and behavior by showing us that a lot of people are doing something.

It's a potent influencer, prompting people to do things from the horrific to the heroic. Almost without exception school shootings happen in bunches. Did you ever notice that? It's because one shooting influences the next perpetrator finally to go through with his twisted plans, too. But on the heroic side social evidence also causes many people to give generously when a natural disaster strikes at home or abroad. Faced with the private choice of whether to write a check, we are nudged in the compassionate direction by hearing about the compassion of so many others. In the end this often results in a superabundance of aid being sent.

As you see, without thinking too much about it, we sometimes tend to do what we see people around us doing. For better or worse, we make a lot of choices based on the crowd. We become products of our environment. We get on the bandwagon, and we conform to our culture.

That dynamic—assimilating and blending and getting rules for living from society rather than from God—is often viewed negatively in Christendom. Often it should be. But also remember that this social evidence principle of human behavior is a neutral principle, one that can be used *for* God's purposes and not just against them. It can save a marriage as quickly as it can slay one. It can spawn a conversion as quickly as it can spoil one.

Social evidence is a neutral principle. It can save a marriage as quickly as it can slay one. It can spawn a conversion as quickly as it can spoil one.

With that in mind, consider it from a biblical perspective.

A Negative and a Positive Example from Scripture

Lest we think that this is some sort of new phenomenon, just recall Old Testament history, in particular, Israel's desire to have its own king (1 Sam. 8). Every nation around it had a king—the Ammonites, the Philistines, the Moabites, you name it. So the people of Israel asked their prophet, Samuel, to petition God on their behalf: Give us a king like the other nations have.

Samuel consulted with God and then told the people it was a stupid idea, but that didn't matter to them. *We want a king!* they insisted. Samuel told them that a king would take away their sons and daughters for his service; that a king would steal their horses, flocks, and land; that a king would be their oppressor, not their liberator. But they were blinded by what others around them were doing:

The people refused to listen to Samuel. "No!"
they said. "We must have a king over us. Then
we'll be like all the other nations: our king will
judge us, go out before us, and fight our battles."
(1 Sam. 8:19–20)

From there, the story line reads like a Shakespearian
tragedy. God granted their new governance structure;
and as you might recall, it was a disaster. The people first
crowned a man named Saul based on his height, strength,
and good looks. Those attributes turned out to be abysmal
predictors of leadership skills. Saul even drafted their sons
and then withheld food from them in the midst of their
battles (1 Sam. 14:24). Sheer genius! In the end Israel
suffered bitter defeats at the hand of the Philistines, and
over the next few centuries, all of Samuel's other prophecies came to pass with many wicked kings gaining control
over the people. Ultimately, Israel lost her sovereignty and
freedom.

Powerful principle, this social evidence, isn't it? More
powerful in this case than authoritative evidence from the
prophet and even from God.

From God's mouth, through his agent's
pen, to our ears, to influence our
behavior: Follow the example of those
who came before you.

Despite the outcome remember that this social evidence principle, like all the principles in this book, is really
a neutral tool that can be used for positive or negative ends.
On the positive side think about how the writer of Hebrews
used it. If you peruse Hebrews 11, you'll see a list of notable
saints from throughout history, a hall of fame of the Judeo-
Christian tradition. The reason for this list? Don't miss

this: It's to provide evidence—social evidence—for the main point the writer wants to make at the beginning of chapter 12. Hebrews 12:1 says:

> Therefore, since we are surrounded by such a
> great cloud of witnesses, let us throw off everything
> that hinders and the sin that so easily entangles,
> and let us run with perseverance the race marked
> out for us. (NIV)

Did you see that? "Since we are surrounded by such a great cloud of witnesses"—since others whom we respect have persevered in faith, let's follow their lead and persevere, as well. From God's mouth, through his agent's pen, to our ears, to influence our behavior: follow the example of those who came before you.

Jesus' Use of Social Evidence

Did you know that Jesus used the same approach as the writer of Hebrews when he preached the greatest sermon ever? He used social evidence to teach one of the hardest lessons of all: embrace persecution; don't run from it.

For sure, it's a lesson taught elsewhere in the New Testament, as we're encouraged to see persecution as inevitable for authentic believers (2 Tim. 3:12; 1 John 3:13; John 15:20), a character-building experience (Rom. 5:3–5; 1 Pet. 1:7), and even a cause for joy! (James 1:2–3; 1 Pet. 4:13). But Jesus pursues a different pathway to persuasion on this topic, at least in his Sermon on the Mount.

Jesus uses social evidence to teach one
of the hardest lessons of all: embrace
persecution; don't run from it.

At the end of the Beatitudes, the cornerstone of his sermon, Jesus is teaching on persecution:

"Blessed are those who are persecuted for righteousness because the kingdom of heaven is theirs. Blessed are you when they insult you and persecute you and falsely say every kind of evil against you because of Me. Be glad and rejoice, because your reward is great in heaven. For that is how they persecuted the prophets who were before you." (Matt. 5:10–12)

It follows the pattern of the Beatitudes, new teachings that we're blessed, not cursed, when we mourn, when we're meek and gentle, when we show mercy to others, and when we're being persecuted. It's a stunning series of reversals, building to a triumphant crescendo: "Be glad and rejoice, because your reward is great in heaven."

If you read closely, though, this is not really where the Matthean version of the Beatitudes ends. Look again at the text. Jesus' teaching actually culminates with this: "For that is how they persecuted the prophets who were before you."

Did you ever pick up on that? Why does Jesus add this point? It almost seems like a throwaway line after his life-changing charge to them to be glad and his promise that their heavenly reward will be worth the pain they're going through.

But it's anything but a throwaway line. I'd suggest that because it's so hard to accept the teaching that we should embrace persecution, Jesus adds a reason beyond reward for us to embrace it, a reason based on social evidence. Jesus knows full well that people are influenced by what others do, and especially by the behavior of those they respect and admire. And he knows that the Old Testament prophets—people like Isaiah, Elijah, Samuel, and Jeremiah—were heroes to the multitudes on the Mount. So what better way to persuade this present generation than to remind them of the experience of the former generation? Embrace persecution not just because of the eternal reward, Jesus says, but also to imitate your courageous ancestors, who were persecuted in the same way.

Think of the impact of Jesus' words. It's truly an aha moment for the original audience. You can practically see the lightbulbs illuminating above their heads all over the countryside. This persecution is awful, but there may be a larger purpose for it. The proof is in the prophets! So maybe I can cope with this situation after all.

It's Not Just for Kids

As you might be thinking, the principle is especially relevant in our kids' lives, steeped as they are in daily peer pressure. It helps us to understand a primary driver of their values and prompts us to get them around peers whose values are consistent with God's. This is one of the upsides of social evidence.

But make no mistake. Social evidence shapes our behavior long after our skin clears up. Almost as much as our teenagers, we adults often choose our paths based on where other people's footprints are.

Indeed, that can be a bad thing. Paul quotes a saying of his day to emphasize that essential truth: "'Bad company corrupts good character'" (1 Cor. 15:33 NIV). As we've seen, though, we can also use this principle wisely and faithfully.

Depending on whom you're trying to influence, you may find that nothing changes their mind more quickly than social evidence—the fact that "other people" are engaging in the course of action you're suggesting. And here's a helpful tip, linking back to the similarity concept we covered in Principle 4: the more similar these other people are to the person you're trying to persuade, the more likely that person will be persuaded. So look hard for these connections; and when you find them, like Jesus, use that information for God's purposes.

For Reflection

The "social evidence" principle says that we tend to do what we see people around us doing. Where have you seen this principle in operation? Have you been influenced by the fact that other people are doing what you're thinking of doing? Make some notes about changes in your behavior, idea, belief, or knowledge as a result of observing or hearing about what others believed or did.

Think about the greatest influence challenge or challenges in your life. Ask yourself this: whom do I know who is doing or believing what I want my influence challenge to do? Think especially of people who are similar to him or her. Plan to use them as examples and impetus for the person you're counseling to change his or her behavior or attitudes.

PART 5

Turn Up the Heat

Thus far in the book we've moved from "pre-influence" principles that we can use before ever saying a word (Principles 1–3), to relationship-building principles that lay the groundwork to speak meaningfully into someone's life (Principles 4–6), to reframing principles that change the way people think (Principles 7–9), to offering compelling evidence to support what we're saying (Principles 10–12). The last three principles also lace together with a common thread: they each entail exerting some sort of pressure to persuade.

I recognize that at first such a statement may sound a bit odd, even wrong. Pressuring people has a negative connotation, and it's easy to consider it an unloving, heavy-handed, and inappropriate means to an end. A lot of times it is, and I'll be the first to tell you that I don't think the Bible teaches it as an approach of first resort. But as I researched the life of Jesus for this book, it became clear to me that there's a time and a place for turning up the heat on someone since that's exactly what Jesus did during his ministry here on earth.

I am confident that we should do what Jesus did so the three persuasion principles in the last section of this book should, in fact, be normative for us Christians. We can *build coalitions*; we can *create, communicate, and carry out consequences*; and we can *limit the availability* of options offered.

As always, though, we have to use these principles with right motives and within appropriate boundaries. God wants us to be influencers, and he wants us to do that his way rather than our own way. Our task is to separate the former way from the latter.

—PRINCIPLE 13 —

Build a Coalition

Conflict. It's inevitable in any relationship. No matter who's involved or how reasonable people are, eventually conflict happens.

Maybe that's why Jesus taught us directly what to do in the midst of interpersonal conflict, even going so far as to offer us a step-by-step conflict resolution process. One of those steps is an influence principle that is closely related to the previous one we've studied.

Let's look at Jesus' teaching on the subject:

> "If your brother sins against you, go and rebuke him in private. If he listens to you, you have won your brother. But if he won't listen, take one or two more with you, so that by the testimony of two or three witnesses every fact may be established. If he pays no attention to them, tell the church. But if he doesn't pay attention even to the church, let him be like an unbeliever and a tax collector to you." (Matt. 18:15–17)

How are we to influence this person to change his mind? First, go to him privately. If that doesn't work—and a lot of times it doesn't—then Jesus says it's appropriate (arguably even mandated) to take a person or two with you to support what you are saying. In other words, to use contemporary language, "build a coalition," a group of like-minded people who come together for a particular cause.

Interestingly, Jesus is not teaching something new here but something very old. This coalition approach is deeply rooted in Jewish tradition, a tradition that says corroboration is essential evidence. Deuteronomy 19:15 illustrates:

> One witness cannot establish any wrongdoing or sin against a person, whatever that person has done. A fact must be established by the testimony of two or three witnesses.

Connecting the dots to influence, then, we take away this lesson: Sometimes the word of one person is not enough; a coalition of at least two or three is required to make a compelling case. This is why, for example, Jesus did not send out the disciples alone to evangelize, but instead he sent them in pairs (see Luke 9:1–6; Mark 6:7). They could have covered more ground as twelve individuals, but they effected greater change as six coalitions. The practice continued in the infant church also, as we see in the book of Acts (e.g., 13:2; 15:27, 39–44; 17:14; 19:22).

Sometimes the word of one person is not enough. Jesus says that a coalition of at least two or three may be required to make a compelling case.

If you'll think back to Principle 12, use social evidence, you'll no doubt see some overlap here. Building a coalition is simply a special case of social evidence. But by its very nature, a coalition puts pressure on the person, group, or organization you're seeking to persuade. That's why it's appropriate for grouping with the last three principles, those that ethically turn up the heat on the target of our influence.

Before we return to another example from Jesus, let's understand the principle a little better by looking at some contemporary examples of how coalitions effect change.

Contemporary Coalitions

- You'd like to remove an adult bookstore from a community.
- You'd like a tenured teacher to change her ways or be removed.
- You'd like a company to stop advancing some anti-Christian cause.
- You'd like your boss to stop making rude and offensive remarks to women.
- You'd like Congress to pass a new law.

In each of these situations, and in dozens of others, you may be powerless to effect change on your own. The person or entity you want to influence simply has too much power. But through joining forces with other like-minded people, you can neutralize that power disadvantage.

Indeed, building a coalition is a more heavy-handed approach to influence than others we've studied up to this point, one that's likely to create conflict before it resolves conflict, but there are times when that's necessary. Sometimes God calls Christians to shake things up and to take a more direct, more insistent, more united approach to effecting change.

Sometimes God calls Christians to shake things up and to take a more direct, more insistent, more united approach to effecting change.

Consider, for instance, the situation involving unequal treatment of people because of the color of their skin. Whether it was the United States in the 1850s or 1960s or South Africa in the 1980s, individuals, no matter how passionate they were, required the assistance of others to achieve justice and change. So an antislavery movement, a civil rights movement, and an antiapartheid movement were launched to push through much needed reforms. In light of the odds, it's hard to imagine success without the coalition approach.

On a more localized scale, Christians have banded together in state after state to put an amendment on the ballot to define marriage as a union between one man and one woman. Petitions brimming with names make their way to the statehouses, culminating in ballot initiatives and almost always a victory for traditional values. It's influence that's simply not possible without the power of numbers.

And on an even more micro scale, you can use the same principle on any given day. A coalition of a father and mother, indivisible despite a strong-willed child's protestations, ploys, and pleas, will have more power to change that child's behavior. A group of employees, united and courageous, can topple the sexual harassment habit of a troglodyte boss. A bold group of believers, picket posters and prayer books in hand, can save babies' lives at the local abortion clinic and maybe even shut down the place.

As you can see, this approach to influence exerts pressure through a collective show of support and/or resources. It's social evidence in action, often backed by some implicit consequence for refusal to change. It's not usually strategy of first resort, but it is something we can pull from our arsenal when other means fail or when our power is less than the power of those we're trying to influence.

Jesus' Coalition

Two thousands years ago a man built a small coalition that would continue his ministry after his early death.
None of these men had much education, and few were
naturally gifted in oratory, evangelism, or ministry management; but collectively, fueled by the Holy Spirit, they
changed the trajectory of history by changing countless
lives, including yours and mine.

> There's simply too much at stake to cede
> this influence method—a method Jesus
> himself taught and applied—to groups
> who would undermine God's purposes.

You may have never thought about it this way, but
we Christians are the fruit of Jesus' coalition-building
approach to influencing the world, so at the very least we
should remain mindful of this pathway to persuasion.

Indeed, coalition building is a pressure-laden approach
to influence, one that can seem uncomfortable because
it initially escalates rather than eliminates conflict, but
the reality is that there's a time and a place for its faithful use. We live in a culture of daily battles for the hearts
and minds of people, and there's simply too much at stake
to cede this influence method—a method Jesus himself
taught and applied—to groups who would undermine his
purposes.

For Reflection

The "build a coalition" principle says that when we're
trying to influence people, there's power in numbers.
Where have you seen this principle in operation? Take a

few minutes to jot down some notes about times when you may have been part of a coalition at work, at your church, or in the community. What were those times, and were they successful?

Think about the greatest influence challenge or challenges in your life. Ask yourself this: Can I assemble some other people to join me in this attempt to influence? Who might they be?

— PRINCIPLE 14 —

Create, Communicate, and Carry Out Consequences

Behavior has consequences.

That's a pretty elementary statement, but simplicity notwithstanding, it has the power to change individuals, families, workplaces, churches, schools, communities, and even entire cultures—if, that is, the linkage actually exists: if positive behaviors do in fact lead to positive consequences and negative behaviors lead to negative consequences.

You don't need a Ph.D. in psychology to know that. We've all seen this sort of cause and effect since childhood, since that fateful day when we had our favorite toy confiscated because we threw it at our younger brother.

Whoops, sorry. Old ghosts. Anyway, for the record, those who do have psychology doctorates call this *operant conditioning*, a process by which the results of a person's behavior influence the likelihood of that behavior being repeated in the future. And even if you don't remember the technical term, remembering the cause-and-effect concept will make you a more effective influencer this very day.

Think that's easy? Or that everybody knows it and everybody does it? Then why are there so many spoiled kids out there, expecting the world to revolve around them and pitching a fit every time it does not? Few consequences for misbehavior. Why are there so many abusive spouses, perpetrating their terror for years? Few consequences for misbehavior. Why is there more crime in some areas of the world than others? In large part fewer consequences for misbehavior. Why do so many workers give lousy service to customers year after year? Same answer.

You could probably add a dozen more examples from your own experience. The behavior-consequence connection is that ubiquitous. For good and for ill, it drives people's choices and actions; as such, it's an essential influence principle for our tool kit.

How Jesus, Paul, and John Used This Principle

Some object that it's unchristian to pressure people this way. Isn't it contrary to the royal law of love, they argue? Isn't it simply wrong to influence through fear and retribution? After all, that's exactly what the abusive spouse is trying to do!

I can understand their objection, and it's worth remembering. It's certainly possible to dishonor God through the misuse of this principle. Unfortunately, we see that misuse far too much, even in the Christian community. But "creating, communicating, and carrying out consequences" is *not* an off-limits or sinful approach to influence. We know this because Jesus himself used it to great effect.

"Creating, communicating, and carrying out consequences" is *not* an off-limits or sinful approach to influence. We know this because Jesus himself used it to great effect.

Nobody particularly likes Scripture passages about hell, but nobody can deny their prevalence. Jesus talked about hell a lot. And he did so in the bluntest of terms. According to Jesus' exact words, when we live an eternity apart from God, we're in a place of eternal fire (Matt. 25:41) and eternal punishment (25:46), a place of agony and torment (Luke 16:25, 28), a place of weeping and gnashing of teeth (Matt. 13:42), and a place where "their worm does not die, and the fire is not quenched" (Mark 9:44).

Clearly Jesus is not one to sugarcoat. He doesn't worry about communicating an unpopular message. To do so would violate the essence of who he is and of who he wants us to be. Rather, the clear message that Jesus taught about the afterlife is that we risk a horrific and eternal penalty if we don't rely on his sacrifice to rescue us. And because of that message—because God created, communicated, and carries out consequences—billions of people throughout the centuries have accepted his free gift. *That's* influence.

My inference from Jesus' approach is that it's entirely legitimate from a biblical standpoint to communicate that behavior has consequences, and it's also biblically consistent to follow through on those consequences.

When the Corinthians were tolerating a professed Christian in their congregation who was having a sexual relationship with his stepmother, Paul was direct and unequivocal: *Expel this guy!*

Apostles like Paul and John seemed to infer the same thing. Paul did this often, but consider just this one example. When the Corinthians were tolerating a professed Christian in their congregation who was having a sexual relationship with his stepmother, Paul was direct and unequivocal: *Expel this guy! What in the world are you thinking? Are you so open-minded that you have nothing but air between your ears? Don't tolerate this kind of immorality today or ever!*

Paul's bottom line to this infant church: this man's behavior must have consequences.

Similarly, when a prideful guy named Diotrephes was bad-mouthing the apostle John, he was quick to address it. Being John, he was slightly subtler than Paul, but he used the same influence principle nonetheless: "I wrote to the church, but Diotrephes, who loves to be first, will have nothing to do with us. So if I come, I will call attention to what he is doing, gossiping maliciously about us" (3 John 9–10 NIV). Translation: The next time I'm in town, Buddy, prepare to be publicly rebuked. Your behavior will have consequences.

The Principle in Daily Life

Now building on this biblically-modeled principle, what does this mean as we move from Sunday morning to Monday morning? At home it means that appropriate discipline, *consistently applied*, will "teach a youth about the way he should go" (Prov. 22:6). At work it means that creating an incentive system that rewards the right behaviors and discourages the wrong behaviors will make the organization more effective. On the ball field, it means that having kids run laps or do push-ups for not listening to the coach will lead to better listening. In the church it means that more accountability and encouragement groups will accelerate spiritual growth. In my classroom it means that the time-honored "cold-calling technique" (calling on students who are not participating) causes students to show up to class prepared and to pay more attention while they're there.

This isn't brain surgery, is it? Hardly. In fact, it's probably the easiest principle to understand in this book. So why, then, is the principle applied with far less frequency than it should be? Why do we tolerate disobedient, insubordinate, and inconsiderate behavior from the people God has entrusted to us?

Here's the problem: whether at home, at work, at school, at church, or anywhere else, sometimes it's just easier to let poor behavior slide than to deal with it.

Perhaps because it can be a lot of work to identify appropriate punishments and rewards. Other times it's because we just give up on the execution; it can be time-consuming and exhausting, for example, to follow through on the penalties we've promised, especially when those penalties are relatively new. But the primary obstacle, I suspect, is that we simply don't want to deal with conflict. Whether at home, at work, at school, at church, or anywhere else, it's just easier, we convince ourselves, to let poor behavior slide than to deal with it.

Don't Fall into the Trap of Conflict Avoidance

Let's face it, most of us don't like conflict so we sometimes ignore bad behavior or address it with a mere slap on the wrist. It's just this one time, we reason, and letting things go preserves the relationship. But then we respond the same way the next time. And the time after that. And before we know it, we've adopted a lifestyle of tolerating inappropriate behaviors from our kids, our spouse, our friends, our extended family, our employees, virtually anyone who challenges our standards.

Eventually, though, not confronting the behavior comes back to haunt us. Our frustration builds to such a point that, at the end of our rope, we look for something—*anything*—that can resolve the problem. Robbed of our peace, we experience a bitter irony of our sweep-it-under-the-rug, "relational preservation" approach to conflict: Ultimately, it yields a joyless, broken, or dying relationship.

The solution was at hand the whole time: behavior should have consequences. But the good news is that the solution remains at hand: follow Jesus' cues. And Paul's. And John's. Create, communicate, and carry out consequences for misbehavior. Simple as that. You don't need to be obnoxious about it, just consistent. You don't need to be threatening. And you don't need to raise your voice. If you want more influence with some of the people in your life, you simply need to tap into a biblically-taught, timeless truth of the human condition: Negative consequences lead to fewer negative behaviors, positive consequences lead to more positive behaviors.

For Reflection

The "consequences" principle says that the likelihood of punishment or loss is a powerful influencer. Where have you seen this principle in operation? Have you used it yourself? What were the contexts, and what were the results? Take a few moments to reflect on and to make some notes about times when it seemed to be the only approach that would work or times when you might have employed it to get better results than you did through using other methods.

Think about the greatest influence challenge or challenges in your life. Ask yourself this: can I create or point to negative consequences of refusal to change—consequences that the person or persons will find persuasive?

— PRINCIPLE 15 —

Limit the Availability

One. Two. Three. You better not let me get to five! Four. Four and a half. . . ."

If you've been around parents these days, you've no doubt heard some variation of this as the parent counts down the time the kid has to comply with the parent's directive. When backed up by some sort of credible penalty for having the time run out, it's a system that almost always works.

So it'll come as no surprise to you that this is one of the favorite influence devices in the Zigarelli household. I like things that work, especially when they don't require me to get out of my chair.

Sometimes I do get up in these situations, though—to set the timer on the microwave oven. If one of my dear angels chooses to put me to the test, I often pass that test by letting modern technology do the countdown for me. This is particularly helpful if the kid's task is a longer one, like cleaning his room or getting dressed for school. I set the timer for several minutes and tell him or her that the timer's running. I don't do it a lot; I simply use this approach when they push back in their adorable, temporarily insane way. If they continue to resist, I tell them I'm setting the timer for fewer minutes—and I don't let them know how many. That one almost *never* fails.

An even more powerful variation is to combine this countdown-to-doom method with escalating consequences.

For example, I'll start with a minor penalty—something like a ten-minute time-out for the child's anarchy—and then if I encounter resistance, the time-out simply increases: eleven minutes, twelve minutes, *thirteen* minutes, and so on. By this point, the child is usually on the run. If not, I start counting by fives: fifteen minutes, twenty minutes, twenty-five minutes.

We can use this approach appropriately—
as Jesus used it—to move people onto
God's agenda.

It's not guaranteed to work instantly—in fact, our most strong-willed child holds the current world record, boasting a 443-minute time-out—but it works great most of the time. And honestly, any howls of protest I hear from the kids are measures that I'm doing something right.

The important questions are these: What am I doing right? Why does it influence people when we limit the available time to comply, and how can we use this approach appropriately—as Jesus used it—in other areas of our life to move people onto God's agenda?

How "Limiting the Availability" Works

Frankly, my countdown method is just a spin-off of what we see in advertising all the time. Act now! Limited time offer! One day only! Sale today! Do those words cause something to happen inside of you? Do you ever feel their strange, uncomfortable, magnetic pull? How about if they pertain to a product or service that you were seriously considering purchasing? Feel the tug now? Don't you hate it?

I know I do. I was in the market to buy a house recently; and while we were negotiating for one that we liked a lot, the seller said that two other potential buyers had been through the house twice each in the past week. "Act now!" was his implicit message. "Your window of opportunity is closing." As a result, we signed a contract that day because we really wanted the house. Beyond that, because there was no way for me to disprove his claim about the other buyers, I paid more than I wanted to pay for the house.

You could call this the "limited availability" principle of influence. If you want to motivate somebody to do something, tap into the natural instinct that people have to avoid missing out on something good. When an item or opportunity is scarce, we tend to want it more.

We see this principle in action everywhere. Besides child-rearing, one-day sales, and peddling houses, what about when a salesman tells us that there's only one car in that color on the lot and that it'll be weeks before others come in? We feel that unpleasant urge to get out the checkbook. It happens in school admissions, too, whether college or private primary and secondary schools. Ever hear an admissions officer say that the deadline is fast approaching or that only a few spots are left in the class? The same principle is in action when a girl tries to make a boy jealous by flirting with his friend. Her message to him is, "Your time is running out if you don't change."

People are motivated by the likelihood of loss far more so than they are by the prospect of gaining some sort of benefit.

People are motivated by the likelihood of loss far more so, in fact, than they are by the prospect of gaining some sort of benefit. We hate to lose out on something that might be valuable to us. We hate to have something be inaccessible or lose the freedom to make choices. Urgency wells up inside of us, encouraging us to move and to move quickly.

That's why limiting the availability of something—making it scarce—works so well as an influencer. That's why my kids run when I start counting and why we run when we hear the word *sale*.

Jesus' Use of the Limited Availability Principle

By now, if I've communicated the principle correctly, you should be asking yourself about the ethics of all this. How is putting pressure on people this way possibly consistent with the Christian ideal? It surely seems counterbiblical to squeeze people for a quick decision, whether it's for a limited-edition vehicle or a place for their kids to be educated. It surely seems counterbiblical to leverage jealously for personal gain or to make ourselves scarce so our employees or spouse will appreciate us more.

Indeed, people use this "limit the availability" principle inappropriately all the time. But as with other principles Jesus modeled and that we can use, the problem is *not* with the influence principle per se; it's with how we use it. Limiting the availability is merely a neutral influence tool. What we do with it makes the action right or wrong.

How do I know it might be a legitimate approach? Because Jesus used this very principle, and he used it *where it matters most*: to influence us to spend eternity with him.

Jesus used this very principle, and he used it where it matters most: to influence us to spend eternity with him.

Look at Matthew 24 and 25, for example. Jesus used the principle twice. First, in chapter 24, as he's teaching his disciples about when he'll return to judge the world, he says it could happen at any time. Specifically, he likens his second coming to what happened back in Genesis:

> "Now concerning that day and hour no one knows—neither the angels in heaven, nor the Son—except the Father only. As the days of Noah were, so the coming of the Son of Man will be. For in those days before the flood they were eating and drinking, marrying and giving in marriage, until the day Noah boarded the ark. They didn't know until the flood came and swept them all away. So this is the way the coming of the Son of Man will be: Then two men will be in the field: one will be taken and one left. Two women will be grinding at the mill: one will be taken and one left. . . . This is why you also must be ready, because the Son of Man is coming at an hour you do not expect." (Matt. 24:36–41, 44)

See the limited availability principle in these words? To paraphrase Jesus, "You don't know when I'm coming back. No one knows when I'm coming back. In fact, *I* don't even know when I'm coming back. So the opportunity to turn your life over to me is running out. It's coming to an end. Make the right choice before the clock expires."

That's scary because that's scarcity. But sometimes scary is exactly what we need to break old patterns of behavior and to make God's choices.

You might remember that Jesus didn't just leave it at that. He went on a few lines later to reinforce this teaching, this time combining the storytelling and limited availability principles. In his parable of the Ten Virgins (Matt. 25:1–13), you'll recall that ten women were waiting to go into the wedding banquet, but no one knew when the doors would be opened. As it turned out, they were not permitted access until late in the night, which required them to have oil for their lamps. Five were prepared for that, but the other five had to scramble around to find oil. By the time the latter five had what they needed, the banquet door had been locked, and they missed out on the feast.

Jesus loves us enough to tell us
the truth—to tell us clearly and candidly
that the opportunity to choose to
follow him is limited.

There are a lot of lessons in that parable, but the most germane for our purposes is that we "don't know either the day or the hour" (Matt. 25:13). Time is running out. The opportunity is scarce. Prepare for my arrival now, Jesus says, before it's too late. Everything is at stake.

Jesus loves us enough to tell us the truth—to tell us clearly and candidly that the opportunity to choose to follow him is limited. He loves us enough to use the scarcity principle, no matter how uncomfortable it makes us, because the alternative is infinitely more uncomfortable for us. The same can be true when we use the principle. For the right reasons and with the right heart, it may be exactly the right approach to communicating God's will to someone.

Influence through Exclusivity and Distinctiveness

Before we close, let me share one corollary to this limited availability principle that we also see in Scripture:

exclusivity. Just as people are drawn to scarce things, we are similarly drawn to things that are distinctive.

We usually like one-of-a-kind things. We consider them valuable. Their uniqueness makes them special. That's why, for example, companies emphasize their distinctives. You simply can't get this product or this sort of service anywhere else, they say. Private schools do the same thing to attract students: "highest SAT scores in the county" or "education from a biblical worldview." Even churches stress exclusive benefits, advertising "relevant pulpit messages," "come-as-you-are services," "a place where kids want to bring their parents to church," and other things that may distinguish them. In any context the message is essentially the same: this is an exclusive opportunity for you. As such, it can influence us to make a decision we would not make otherwise.

Indeed, as with some of the other principles, this is an approach that we're prone to misusing, but we can instead use it with integrity and power to advance God's purposes. After all, that's how God set up salvation, isn't it? Did you ever wonder why Jesus is the "One and Only Son" of God (John 3:16)? Why "no one comes to the Father except through Me" (John 14:6)? I think it's because God knows that by design, exclusivity influences us. It stimulates us to action and to make choices we wouldn't otherwise make. So God sent his only begotten Son as the exclusive bridge for all of humanity, to influence the most important decision of our life.

For Reflection

The "limited availability" principle says that if something is scarce, we tend to want it more. Where have you seen this principle in operation? Has it caused you to make a decision about something that you wouldn't otherwise have made? Jot down a couple of examples in your note-book of how it was used and how you responded to it.

Think about the greatest influence challenge or challenges in your life and then respond to the following questions: Is there a way to limit this person's opportunity to do what I'm asking? Or is there a way to demonstrate the distinctiveness of the option I present?

The Influence Planning Work Sheet

When I began to do the research for this book, it was almost out of desperation. I've never been the world's greatest influencer. One of the reasons for that, I've come to understand, is because I had never studied the many biblical approaches to doing this right—to getting good and godly results by using good and godly methods.

Admittedly, I'm still not the world's greatest influencer. There are still a lot of people God's entrusted to me whom I'd like to influence for his purposes. And there are still countless situations where I'd like to see change but where I've had limited success.

I'm making progress, though, in part because I've delved deeply into the biblical art of influence, in part because I've been practicing these techniques and building my skills and in part because for the first time in my life I have a tool that equips me to think through the menu of options at my disposal in any influence situation.

That tool is the Influence Planning Work Sheet that you'll find in the next few pages. I've used it on a number of occasions, as have many of my MBA students, and it's provided a plethora of good ideas for us—ideas that would have never been spawned without the tool. It's also served as a useful guardrail to avoid counterbiblical approaches to persuasion and as an essential reminder that we're to co-labor with God throughout this process (Principle 1) rather than going at it alone.

Let me encourage you to use this work sheet. You can make as many copies of it as you'd like for personal use because you'll want to use it whenever you find yourself with a significant influence challenge. Spending a few minutes with each of the fifteen questions may generate the one idea you need to change *everything* in that situation. And frankly, a lot of times it will take only one fresh idea to achieve real change, real transformation.

Thanks so much for joining me on this journey. If you'd like to continue on and learn more, I'd like to help you with that. I've created a Web site that offers more in-depth information and more examples for each of these fifteen principles. You can also get more copies of the Influence Planning Work Sheet there, as well as some other useful tools.

Please come visit this online resource center when you get a chance at http://www.epiphanyresources.com/Influence. You can also see and purchase the supplemental videos that go with this study by visiting www.lifeway.com/zigarelli.

Influence Planning Work Sheet

The goal: To influence _____

to _____

INFLUENCE PRINCIPLE	A QUESTION TO ASK MYSELF	WHAT I COULD DO
1. Prayer changes things. God responds to our requests for change.	Have I prayed diligently for change?	
2. Be a person others will follow. We're influenced by people whom we like, trust, and respect and who walk the talk.	What characteristics do I need to demonstrate to earn the right to be heard? Also, are there others whom this person likes and trusts who could be the influencers?	
3. Know your audience. The better we understand our audience, the more effectively we can shape our message.	What do I need to know about this person before I choose an influence strategy?	
4. Connect through similarity. We're more easily persuaded by people similar to us than by those who are different.	What do we have in common that could be a starting point for relationship and discussion? Or should I instead work through others who are more similar to this person?	

INFLUENCE PRINCIPLE	A QUESTION TO ASK MYSELF	WHAT I COULD DO
5. Serve their needs. Meeting people's needs and desires makes them more receptive to our requests.	What does this person value that I could give to him or her?	
6. Ask for their opinion. People are more likely to be persuaded if they're part of the process.	Have I asked for this person's solutions and ideas, and have I genuinely listened to them?	
7. Tell a story. Stories persuade because they captivate, inspire, and stay with us.	What stories can I tell that will get my point across in a memorable and emotional way?	
8. Construct a contrast. The difference between things greatly influences our perceptions and decisions.	Is there something to which this option compares favorably? Can I show how much worse things could be?	
9. Find a metaphor. Metaphor—showing that one thing resembles another thing—can cause people to see and think in new ways.	Is there a metaphor I can use that will encourage this person to see the situation differently?	
10. Use authoritative evidence. We're influenced by experts and credentials.	Have I demonstrated my expertise on this matter or pointed to other expert evidence that this person would find convincing?	

INFLUENCE PRINCIPLE	A QUESTION TO ASK MYSELF	WHAT I COULD DO
11. Use experiential evidence. Sometimes we'll never be convinced unless we see it for ourselves.	Can I get this person to personally experience the cost of the status quo or the benefit of change?	
12. Use social evidence. We tend to do what we see people around us doing.	Can I identify other people who are doing what I want this person to do, especially people who are similar to him or her?	
13. Build a coalition. When we're trying to influence people, there's power in numbers.	Can I assemble some other people to join me in this attempt to influence?	
14. Create, communicate, and carry out consequences. The likelihood of punishment or loss is a powerful influencer.	Can I create or point to negative consequences of refusal to change— consequences that this person will find significant?	
15. Limit the availability. If something is scarce, we tend to want it more.	Is there a way to limit this person's opportunity to do what I'm asking? Or is there a way to demonstrate the distinctiveness of this option?	

Notes

Principle 1, Pray for Change

1. "Americans Are More Likely to Base Truth on Feelings," *The Barna Update*, 12 February 2002, www.barna.org.

Principle 3, Know Your Audience

1. *Barna Update*, 24 January 2006, www.barna.org.

Principle 5, Serve Their Needs

1. Diane Contu, "Negotiating without a Net: A Conversation with the NYPD's Dominick J. Misino," *Harvard Business Review*, October 2002, 50–54.

Principle 6, Ask for Their Opinion

1. *Barna Update*, 31 January 2005, www.barna.org.

Principle 7, Tell a Story

1. From Gordon D. Fee and Douglas Stuart, *How to Read the Bible for All Its Worth*, Second Edition (Grand Rapids: Zondervan Publishing, 1993), 147.

NOTES

Notes

NOTES

NOTES

Notes

NOTES

NOTES

NOTES

NOTES

NOTES

NOTES

NOTES

Notes

NOTES